HAL•LEONARD
GUITAR PLAY-ALONG

BRAD PAISLEY

CONTENTS

Cover photo credit: © Gerry Maceda / Retna LTD.

ISBN 978-1-4234-8409-7

HAL•LEONARD®
CORPORATION
7777 W. BLUEMOUND RD. P.O. BOX 13819 MILWAUKEE, WI 53213

Visit Hal Leonard Online at
www.halleonard.com

Alcohol

Words and Music by Brad Paisley

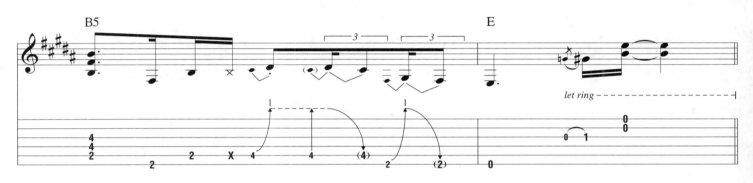

* Brad Paisley's guitars are equiped with a G-bender that allows him to perform many unorthodox passages which have been arranged for standard guitars in this transcription.

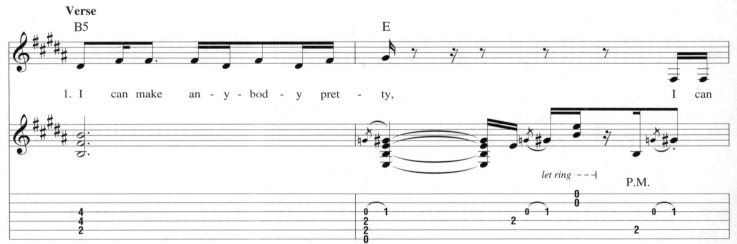

Verse

1. I can make an-y-bod-y pret-ty, I can

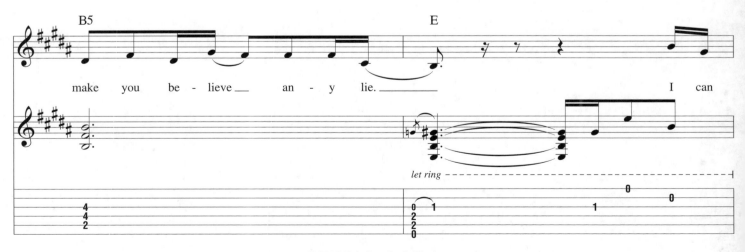

make you be-lieve an-y lie. I can

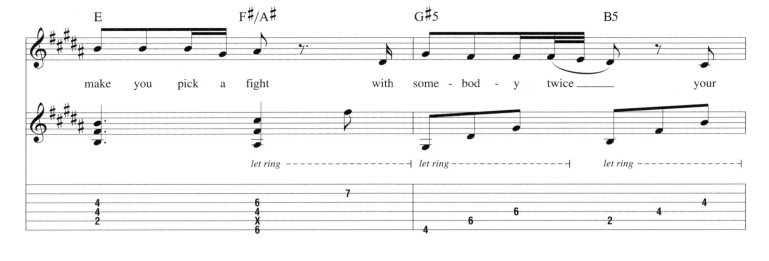

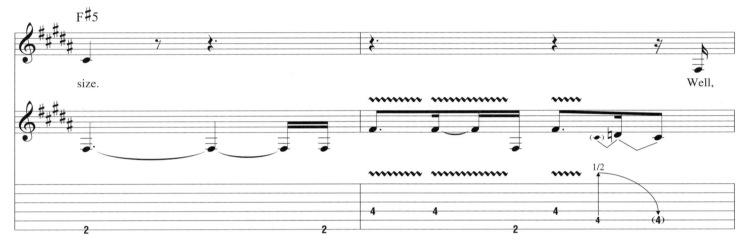

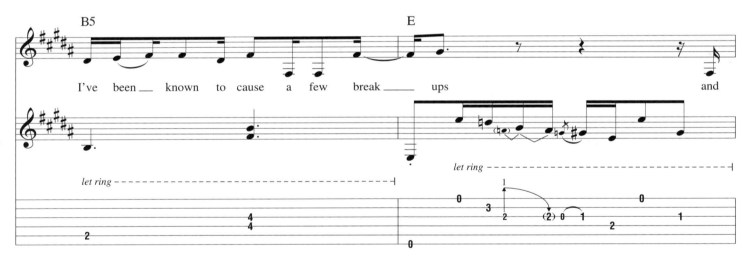

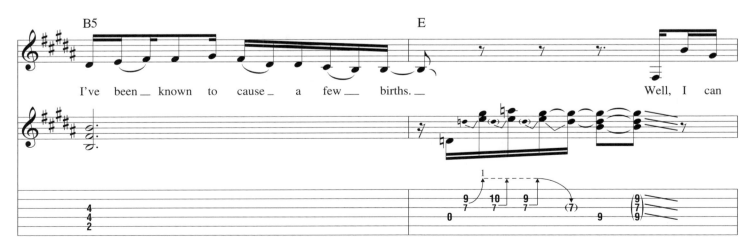

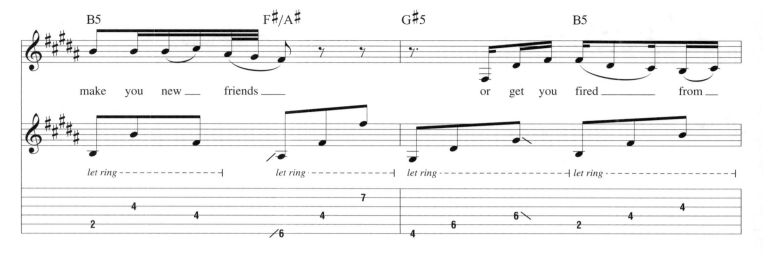

make you new friends or get you fired from

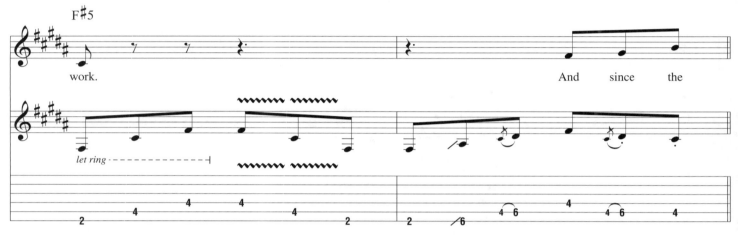

work. And since the

Chorus

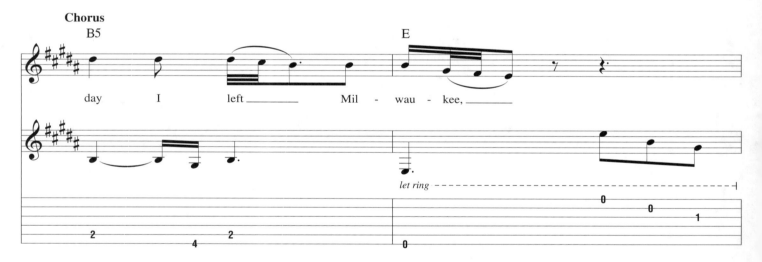

day I left Mil - wau - kee,

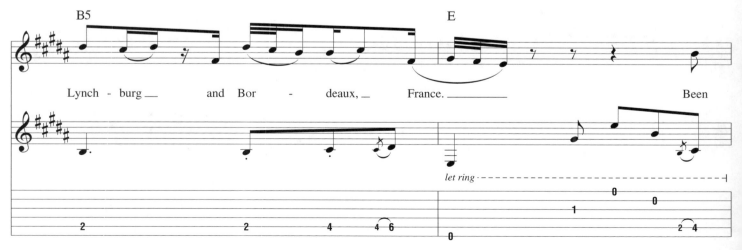

Lynch - burg and Bor - deaux, France. Been

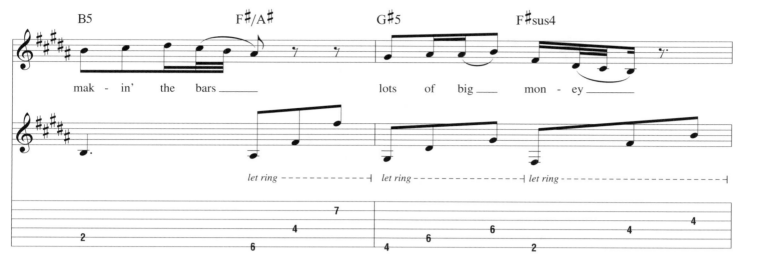

makin' the bars _____ lots of big _____ mon-ey _____

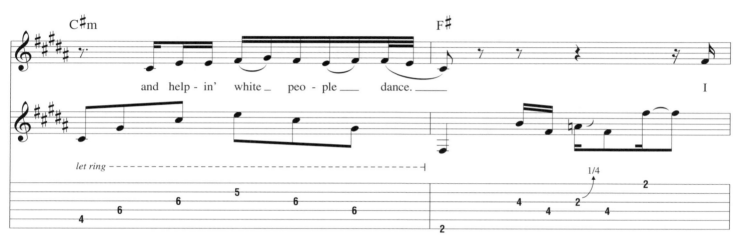

and help-in' white _ peo-ple _____ dance. _____ I

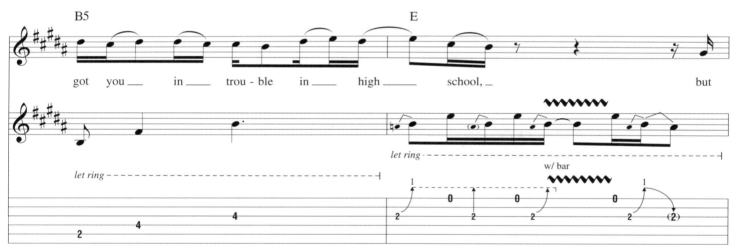

got you _____ in _____ trou-ble in _____ high _____ school, _____ but

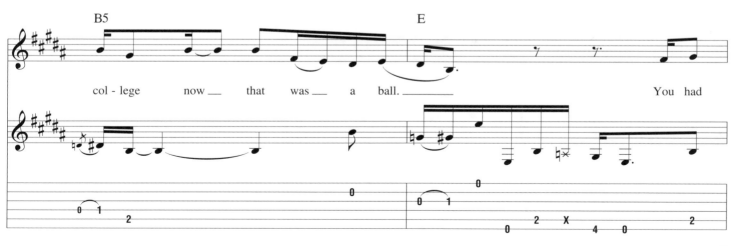

col-lege now _____ that was _____ a ball. _____ You had

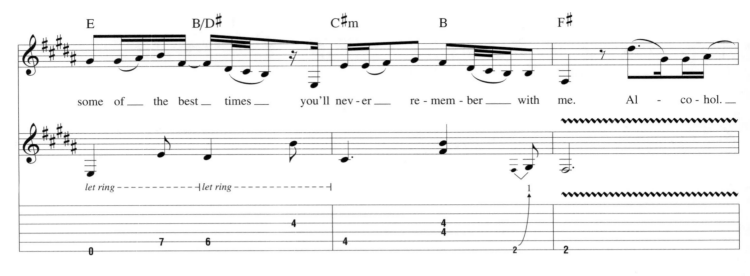

some of ___ the best ___ times ___ you'll nev - er ___ re - mem - ber ___ with me. Al - co - hol. ___

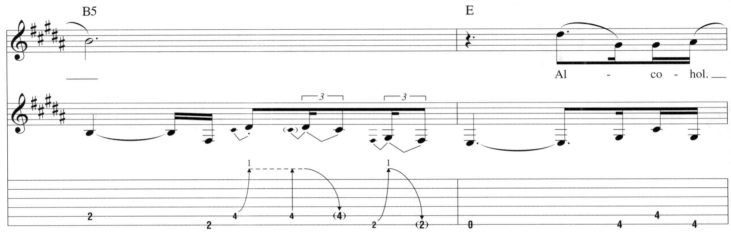

Al - - co - hol.

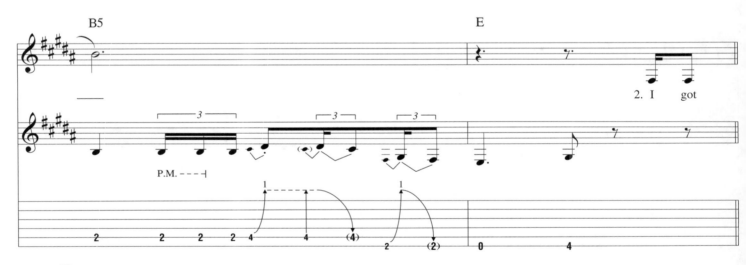

2. I got

Verse

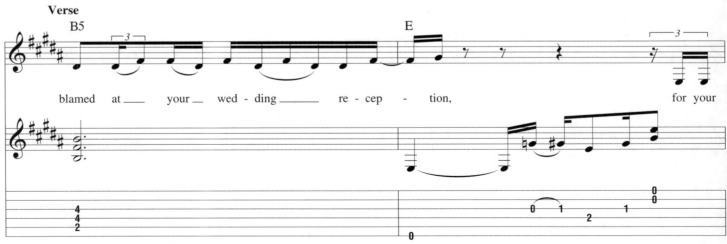

blamed at ___ your ___ wed - ding ___ re - cep - tion, for your

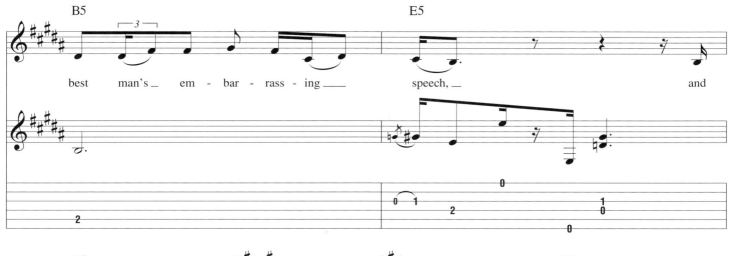

best man's em-bar-rass-ing ___ speech, ___ and

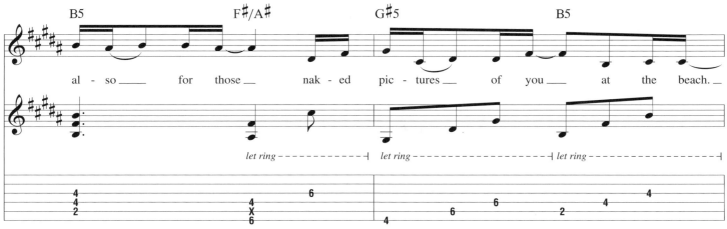

al - so ___ for those ___ nak - ed pic - tures ___ of you ___ at the beach. ___

let ring ------- | *let ring* ------- | *let ring* -------

I've

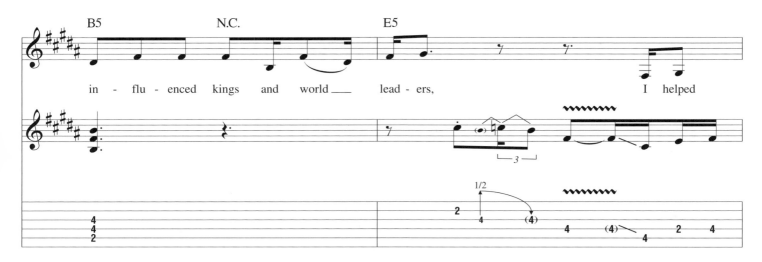

in - flu - enced kings and world ___ lead - ers, I helped

Hem-ing - way __ write like __ he did. __ And I'll bet you __ a drink or two _____ that I _____ can make you __ put that __ lamp-shade on your head. _____ 'Cause since the

Chorus

day I left _____ Mil - wau - kee,

let ring

Lynch - burg ___ and Bor - deaux, ___ France. ___ I been

mak - in' a fool ___ out ___ of folks just like ___ you ___

and help - in' white ___ peo - ple ___ dance. ___ I am

med - i - cine ___ and ___ I am ___ poi - son. ___ I can

help you up — or — make — you fall. —

You had

some of — the best — times — you'll nev - er — re - mem - ber with

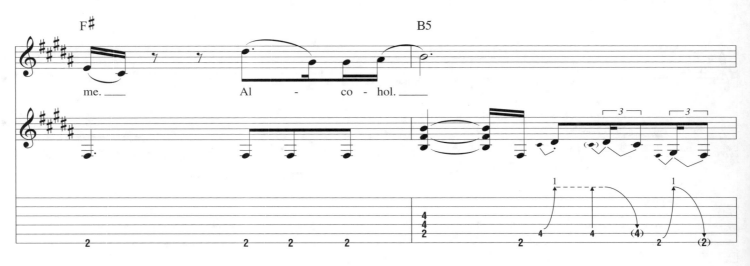

me. — Al - co - hol. —

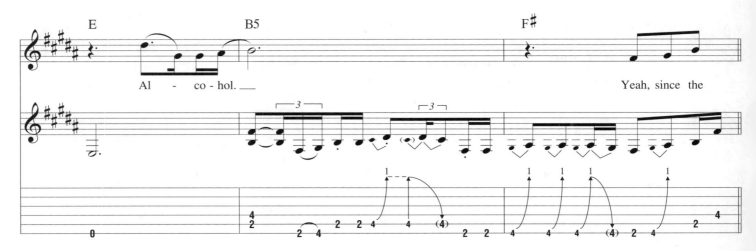

Al - co - hol. —

Yeah, since the

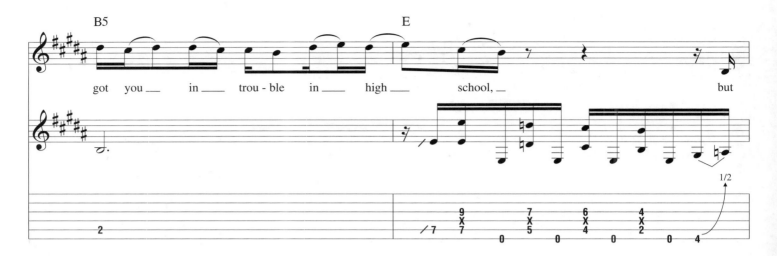

got you ___ in ___ trou-ble in ___ high ___ school, ___ but

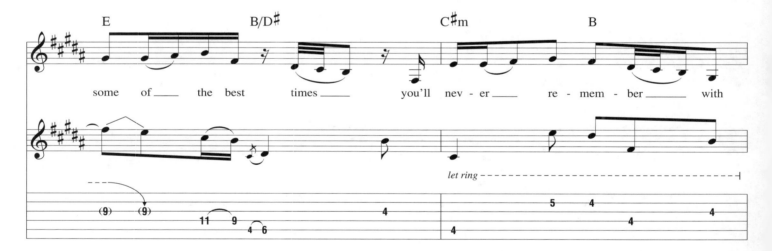

col - lege now ___ that was ___ a ball. ___ You had

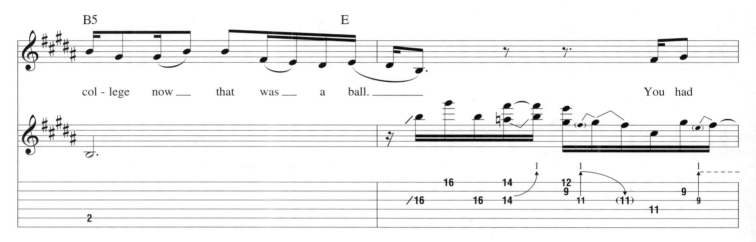

some of ___ the best times ___ you'll nev-er ___ re - mem - ber ___ with

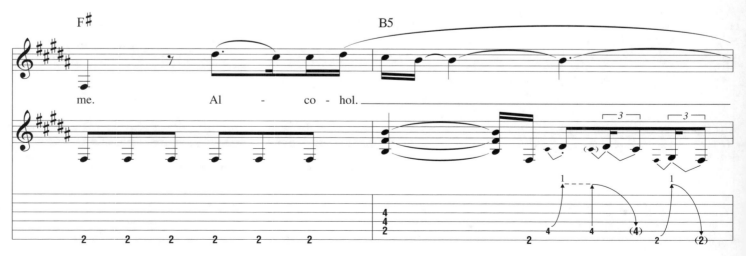

me. ___ Al - co - hol. ___

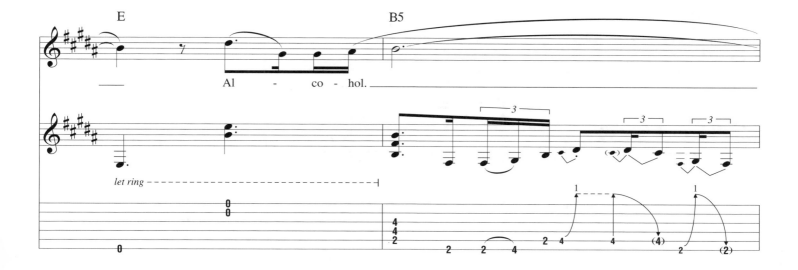

Outro-Guitar Solo

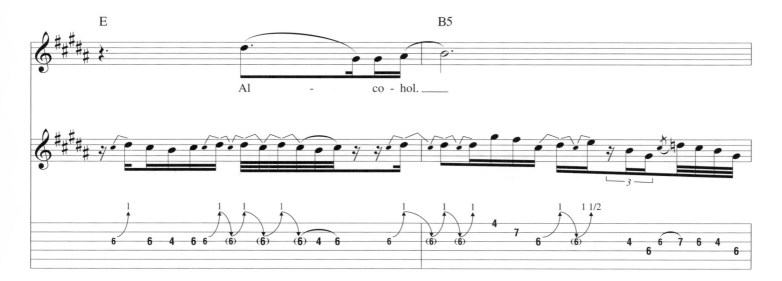

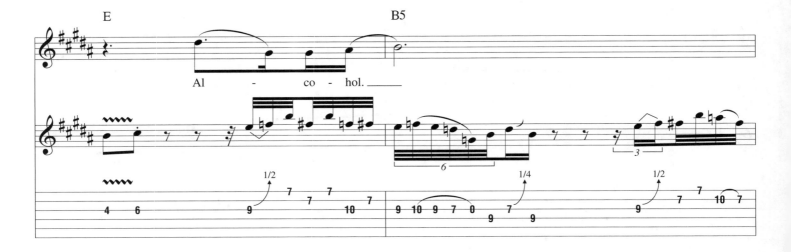

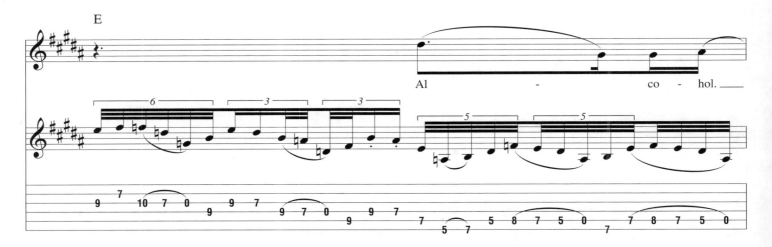

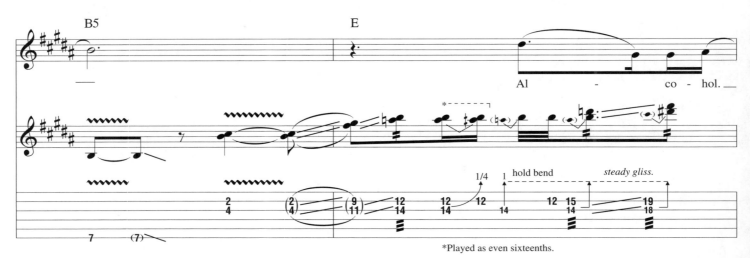

*Played as even sixteenths.

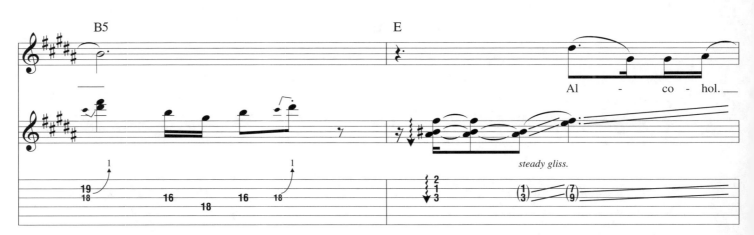

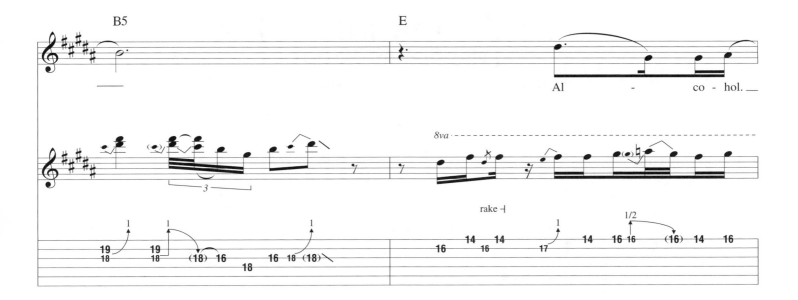

Al - co - hol.

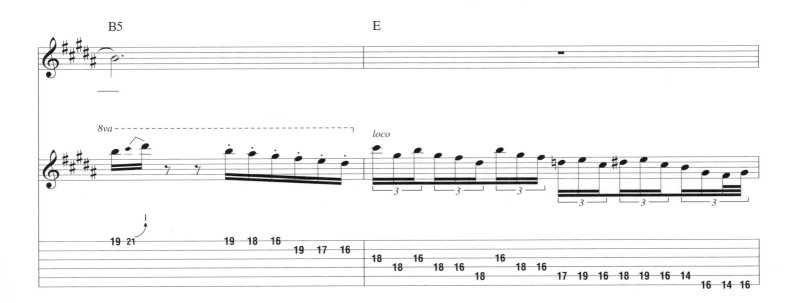

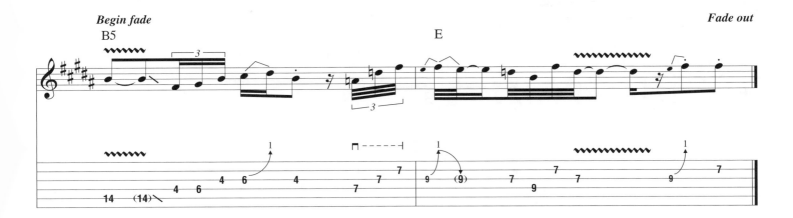

I'm Gonna Miss Her
(The Fishin' Song)

Words and Music by Brad Paisley and Frank Rogers

Capo II

*Symbols in parentheses represent chord names respective to capoed guitar.
Symbols above represent actual sounding chords. Capoed fret is "0" in tab.

1. Well, I love her, ___

but I love to fish. ___ I spend all day ___ out on ___ this lake ___ and

16

Chorus

miss her ___   when I ___ get   home. ___

w/ slight dist.

let ring -

*Chord symbols reflect actual sounding chords.
All tab numbers are actual.

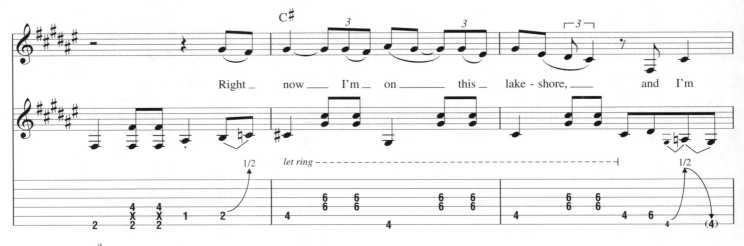

Right ___ now ___ I'm ___ on ___ this ___ lake - shore, ___   and   I'm

let ring -

sit - tin' in   the ___ sun.   I'm sure ___ it -'ll   hit   me ___

let ring -

when I ___ walk through ___ that door to - night. ___   Yeah, ___ I'm ___ gon-na

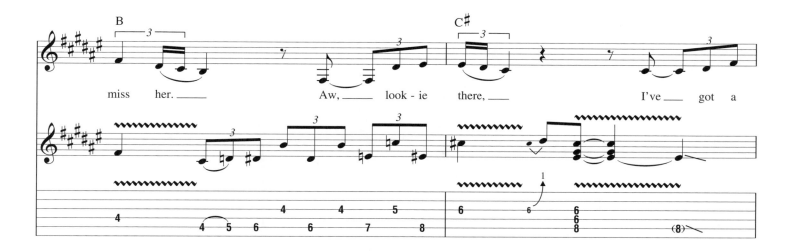

miss her. ___ Aw, ___ look-ie there, ___ I've ___ got a

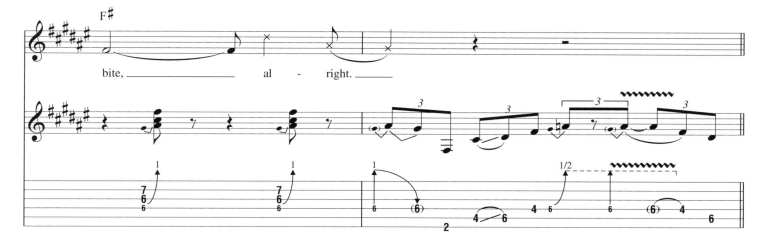

bite, _____ al - right. _____

Guitar Solo

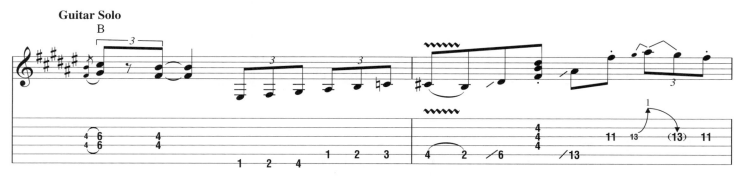

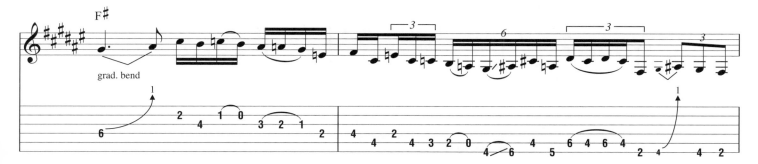

grad. bend

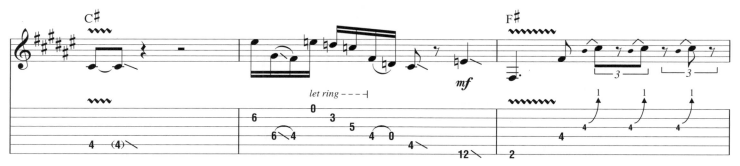

let ring - - - -｜

mf

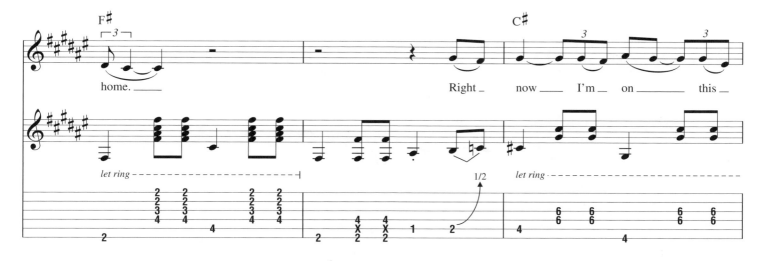

home. _____ Right _ now _____ I'm _ on _____ this _

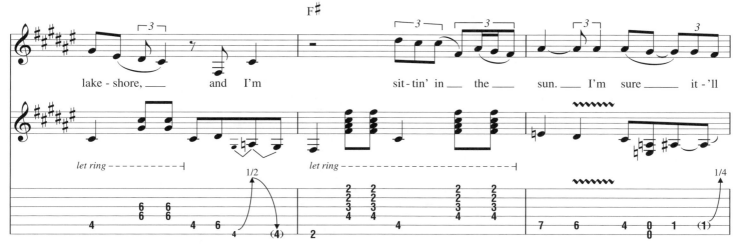

lake - shore, _____ and I'm sit - tin' in the _____ sun. _____ I'm sure _____ it - 'll

hit me _____ when I _____

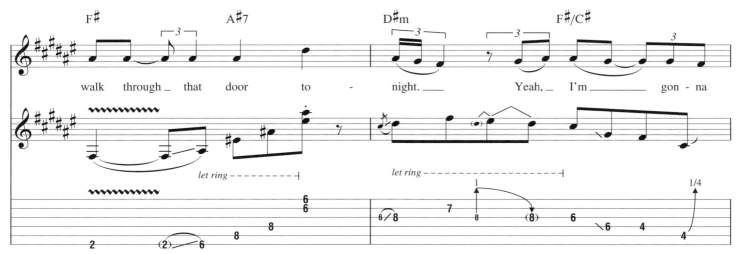

walk through _ that door to - night. _____ Yeah, _ I'm _____ gon - na

miss her. ____ Aw, ___ look - ie there, _____ an - oth - er bite. _

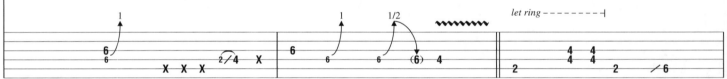

Outro

Yeah, ____ I'm ____ gon - na miss her. ___ Oh, ___ look - ie

Freely

there, _____ I've ___ got a bite. _____

Online

Words and Music by Brad Paisley, Chris DuBois and Kelley Lovelace

dai. ___   I ___ still live with my mom ___ and dad, ___ I'm

five foot three and o - ver - weight. ___   I'm ___ a sci - fi fa - nat - ic, a

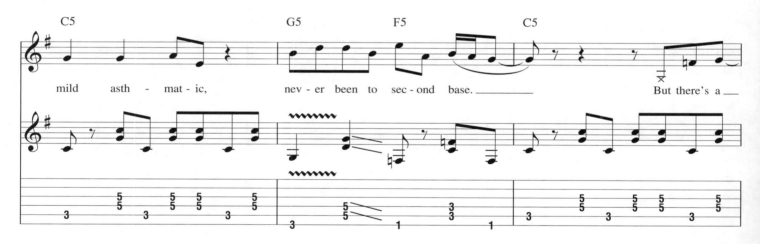

mild asth - mat - ic, nev - er been to sec - ond base. ___   But there's a ___

___ whole 'noth - er me that you need ___ to see. ___ Go check out ___ My - space. ___

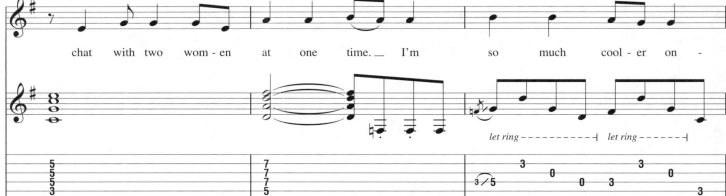

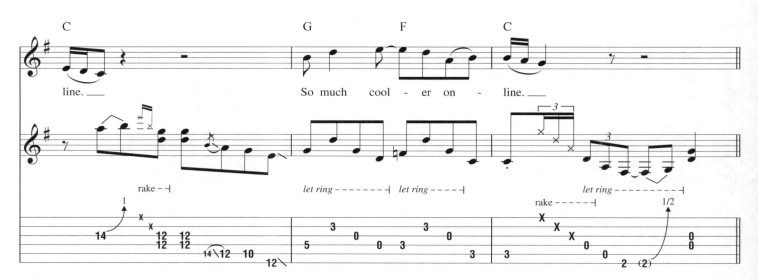

Verse

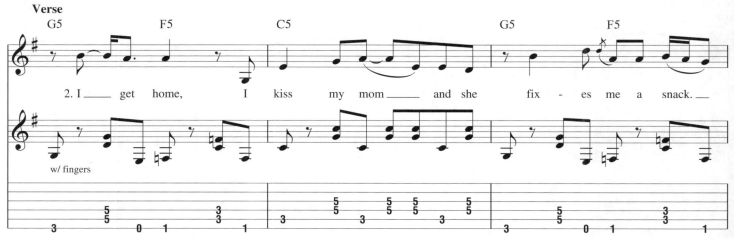

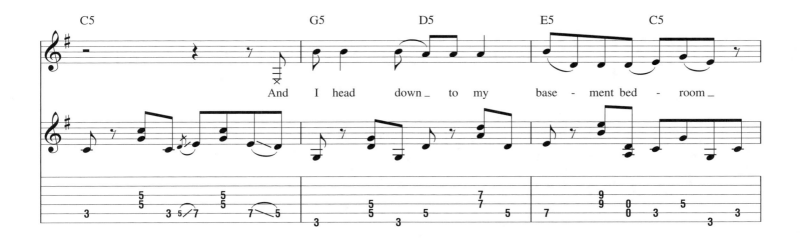

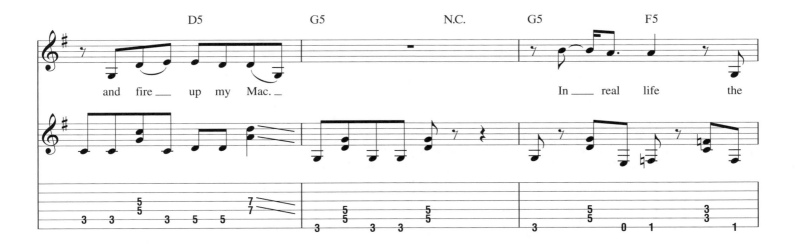

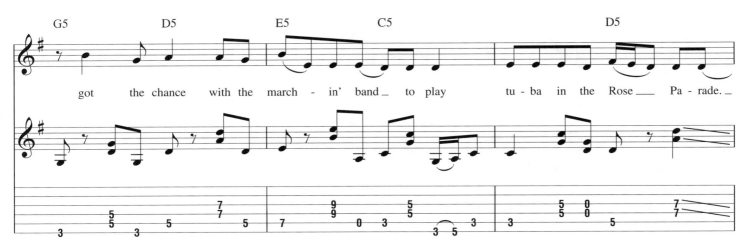

grow an -oth - er foot __ and I lose a bunch of weight __ ev - 'ry time I log in. __

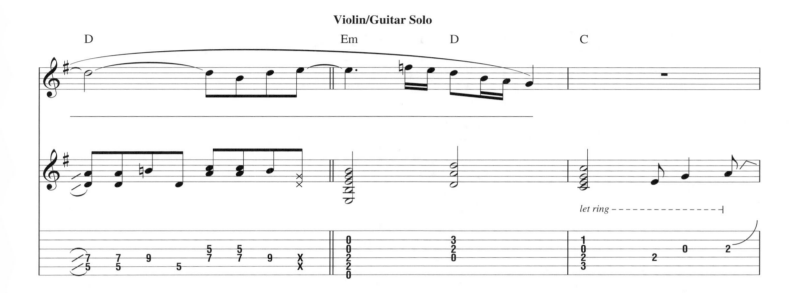

Violin/Guitar Solo

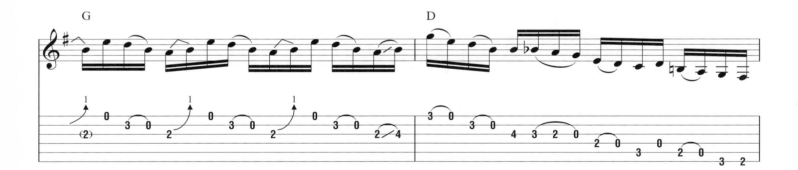

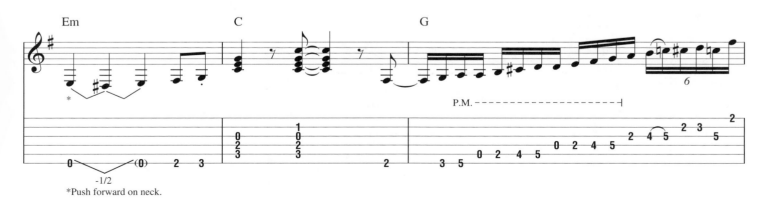

*Push forward on neck.

Yeah, I'm cool-er on - line. ___ Yeah, I'm so much cool-er on -

line. ___ Yeah, I'm cool-er on - line. ___

Guitar Solo

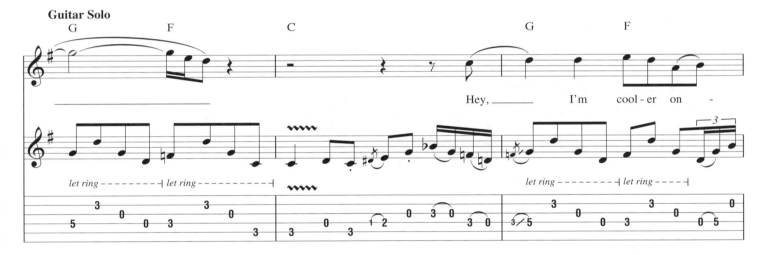

Hey, ___ I'm cool-er on -

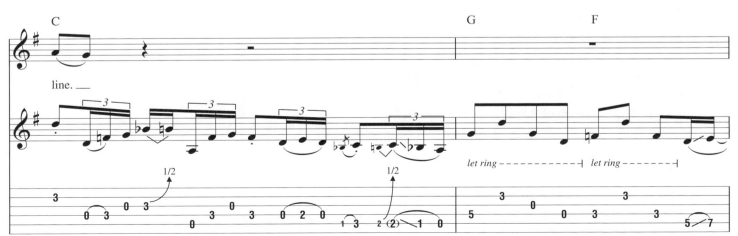

line. ___

Yeah, _____ you ought-a see me on - line. _____

let ring ---------- | *let ring* ----- |

Hey, _____ I'm cool - er on -

- line. _____

*Pull back on neck.

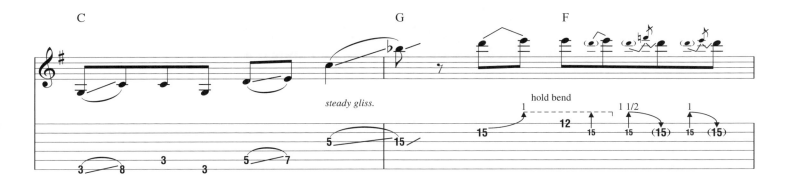

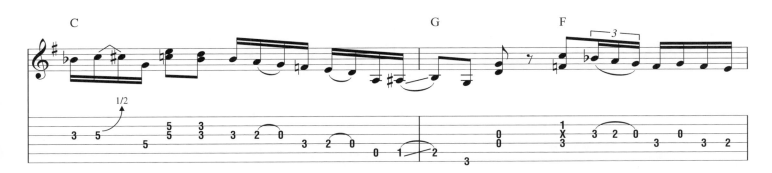

Outro

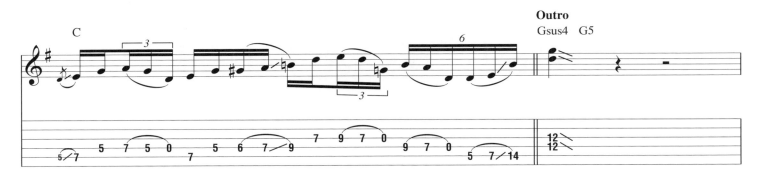

Fade out

Additional Lyrics

Chorus But online I live in Malibu.
I pose for Calvin Klein, I've been in G.Q.
I'm single and I'm rich and I got a set of
Six-pack abs that will blow your mind.
It turns girls on that I'm mysterious.
I tell 'em I don't want nothin' serious.
'Cause even on a slow day I can have a three way
Chat with two women at one time.
I'm so much cooler online.
Yeah, I'm cooler online.

Mud on the Tires

Words and Music by Brad Paisley and Chris DuBois

Capo II

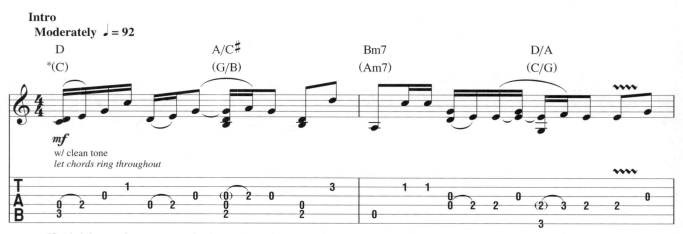

*Symbols in parentheses represent chord names respective to capoed guitar.
Symbols above reflect actual sounding chords. Capoed fret is "0" in tab.

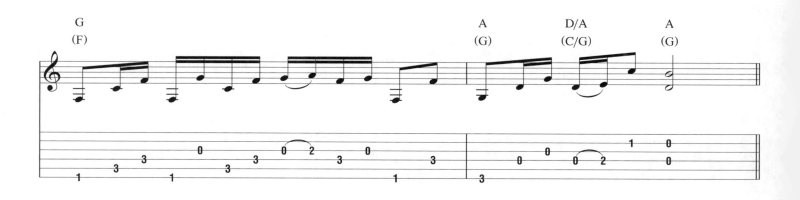

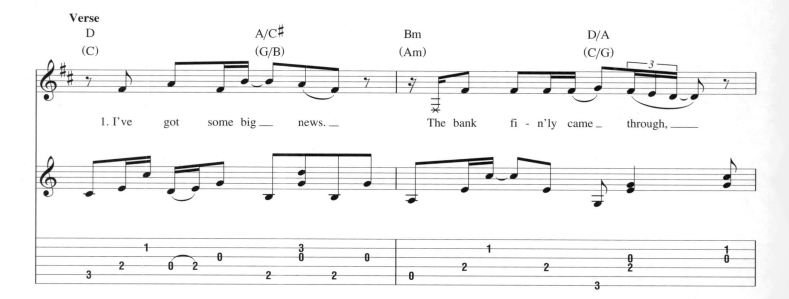

1. I've got some big news. The bank fi-n'ly came through,

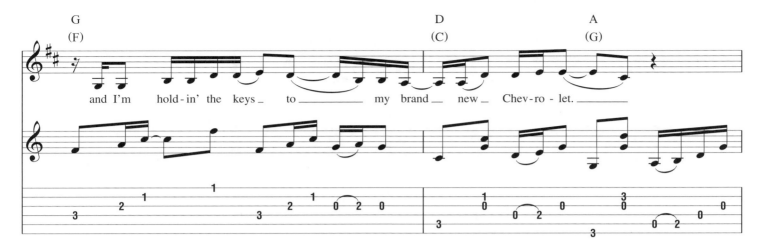

and I'm hold-in' the keys ___ to ___ my brand ___ new ___ Chev-ro-let. ___

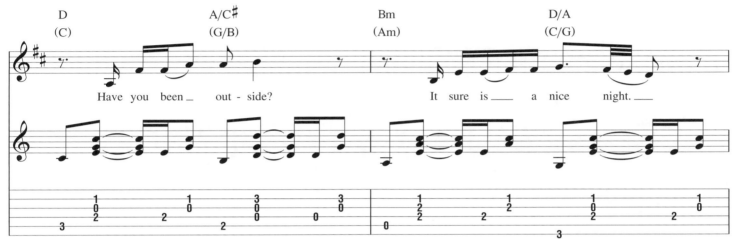

Have you been ___ out-side? It sure is ___ a nice night. ___

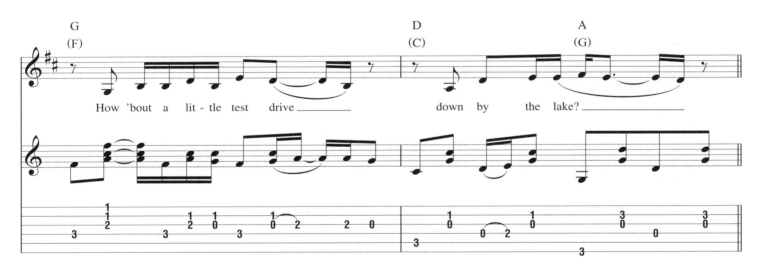

How 'bout a lit-tle test drive ___ down by the lake? ___

Pre-Chorus

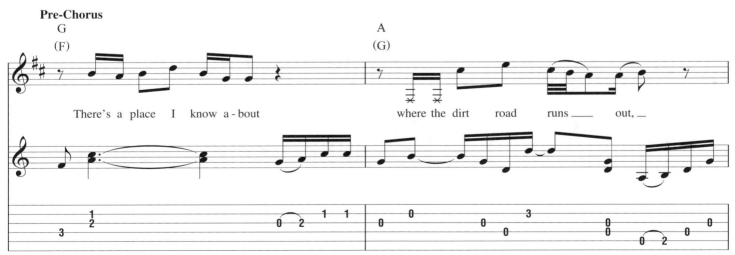

There's a place I know a-bout where the dirt road runs ___ out, ___

we can try out   the four-wheel   drive.

Come on __ now, _ what do ya say? _____   Girl, I   can hard - ly   wait _____

to get a lit - tle mud on __ the tires. _____   'Cause it's   a good __

Chorus

___ night _____   to be out __ there   soak - in' up __   the moon-

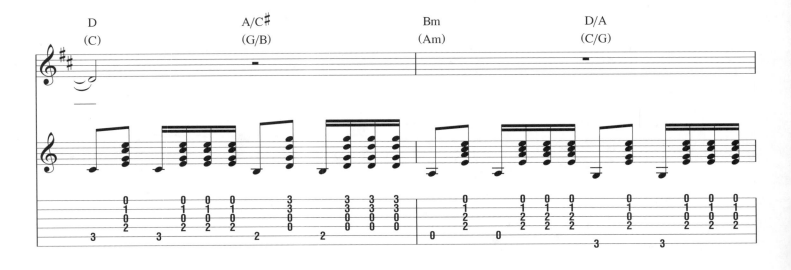

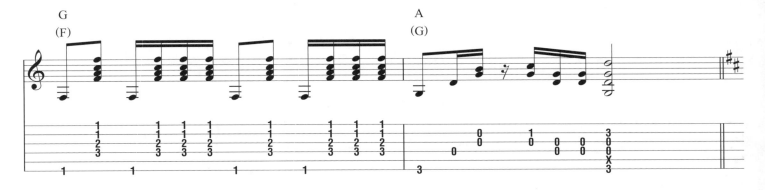

Verse

2. Moon-light on a duck blind, cat-fish on a trot-line.

remove capo

w/ slight dist.

*Chord symbols reflect actual sounding chords. All tab numbers are actual.

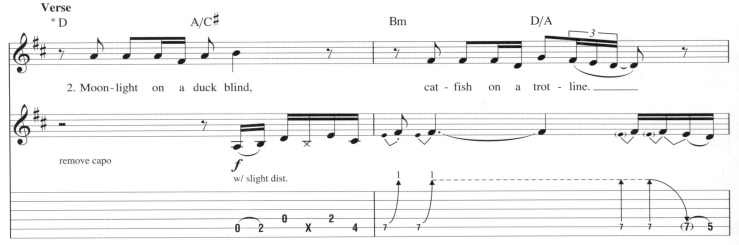

Sun - set's a - bout nine this time of year.

let ring

let ring

38

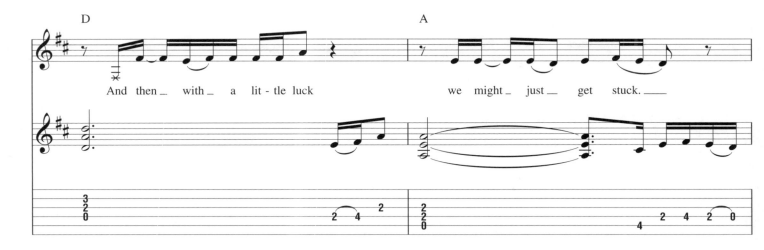

And then _ with _ a lit-tle luck   we might _ just _ get stuck. _

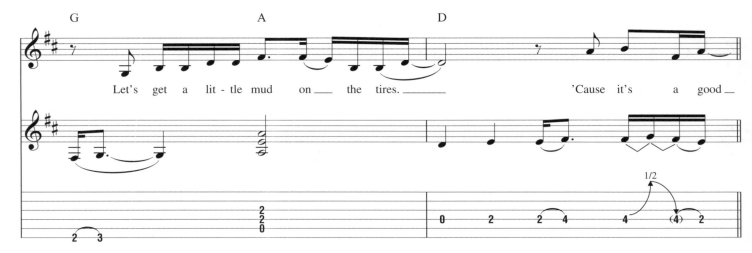

Let's get a lit-tle mud on _ the tires. _   'Cause it's a good _

Chorus

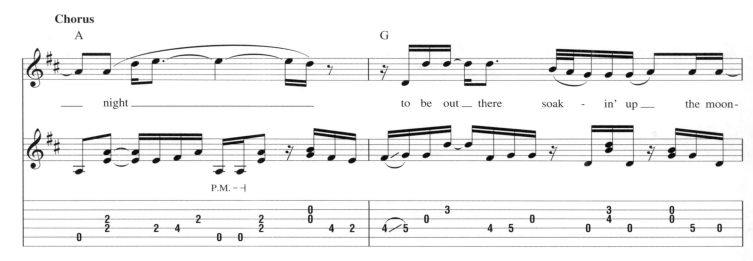

_ night _   to be out _ there soak - in' up _ the moon-

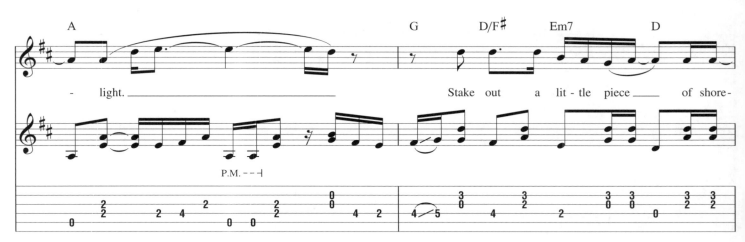

- light. _   Stake out a lit - tle piece _ of shore-

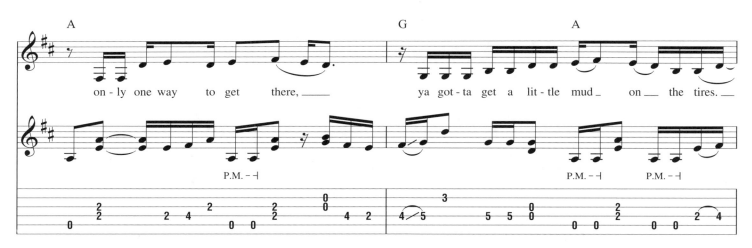

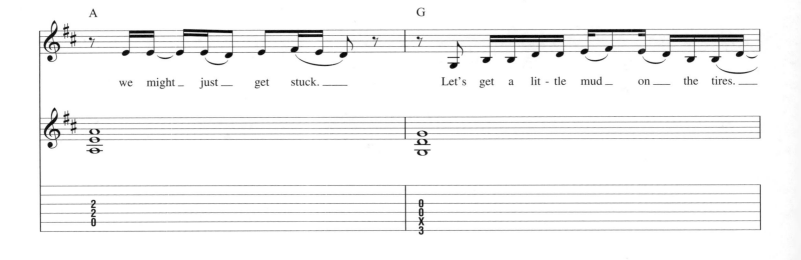

we might _ just _ get stuck. _ Let's get a lit - tle mud _ on _ the tires. _

Outro-Guitar Solo

A

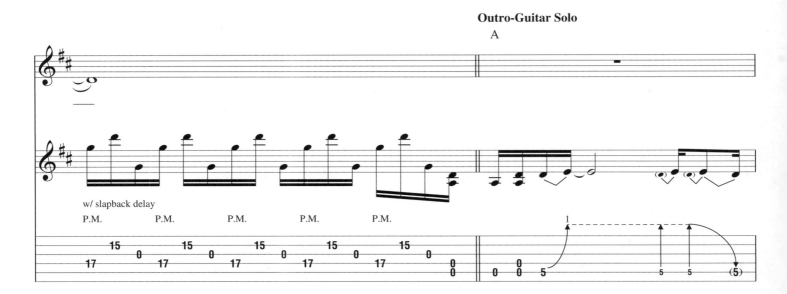

w/ slapback delay

P.M. P.M. P.M. P.M. P.M.

G   A

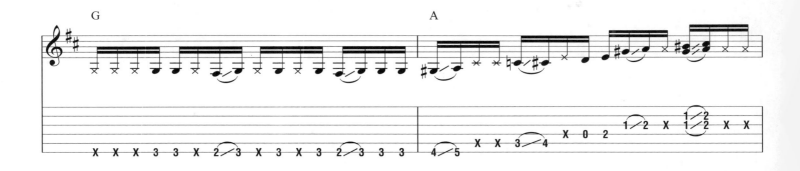

G   D/F#   Em7   D

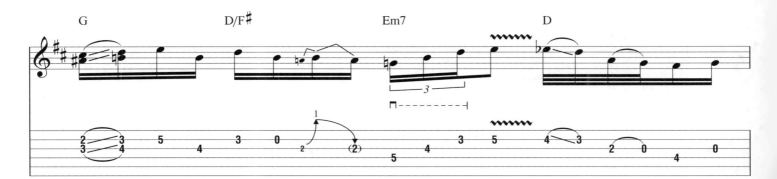

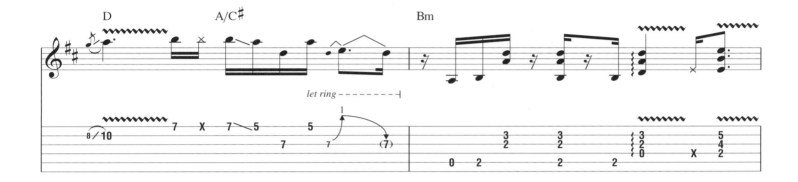

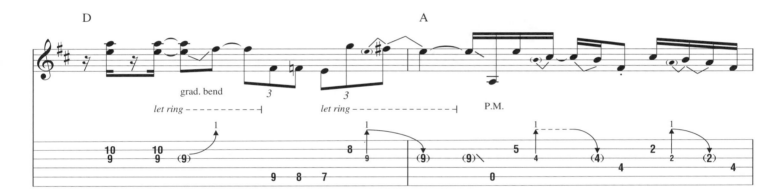

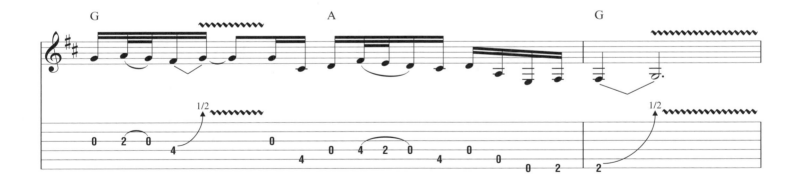

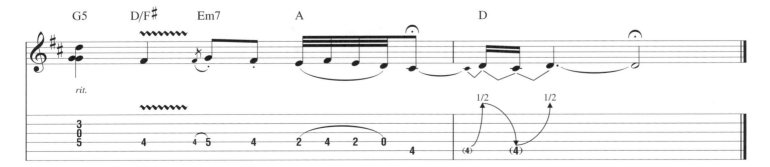

Start a Band

Words and Music by Kelley Lovelace, Ashley Gorley and Dallas Davidson

Intro
Moderately ♩ = 122

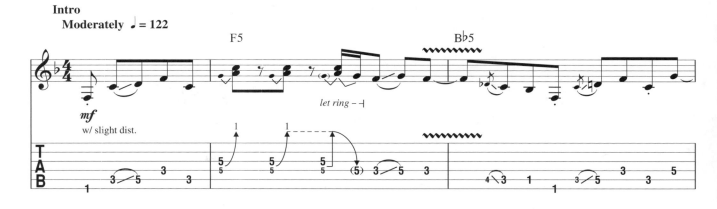

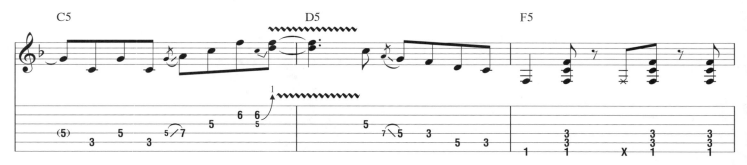

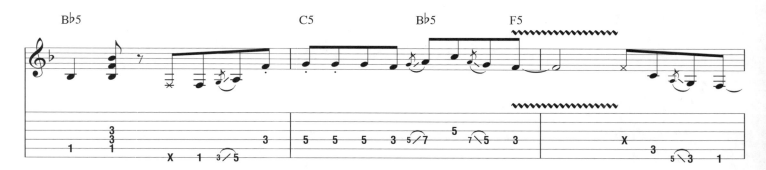

Verse

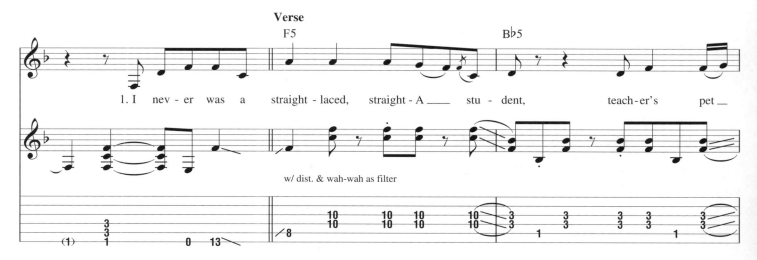

1. I nev-er was a straight-laced, straight-A ___ stu-dent, teach-er's pet ___

w/ dist. & wah-wah as filter

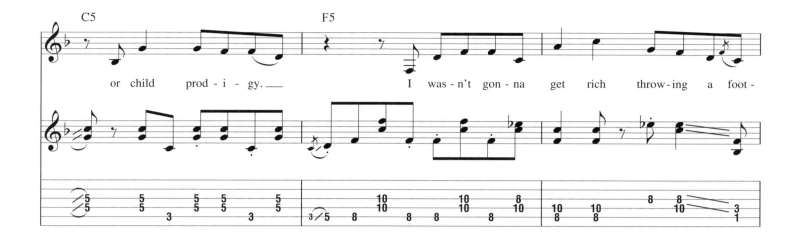

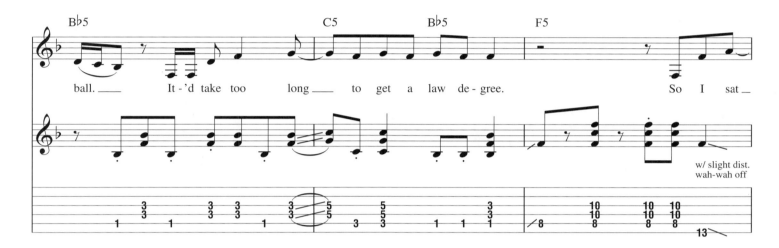

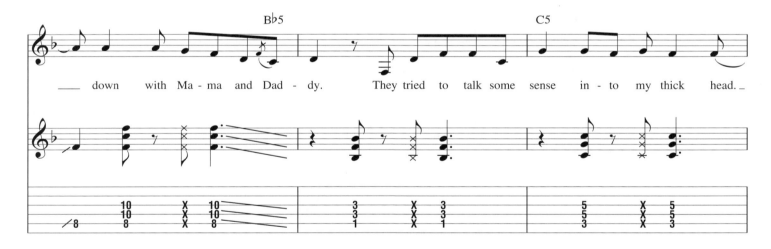

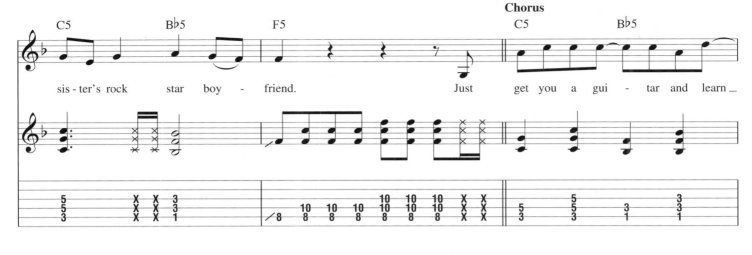

sis - ter's rock star boy - friend. Just get you a gui - tar and learn

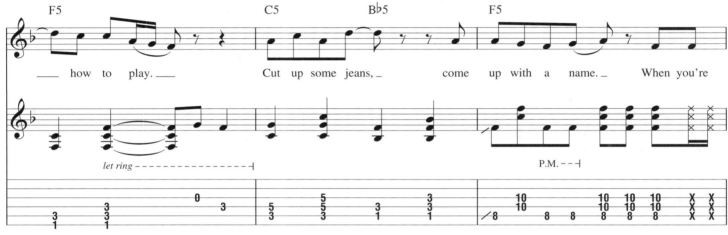

how to play. Cut up some jeans, come up with a name. When you're

liv - ing in a world that you don't un - der - stand, find a few good bud - dies,

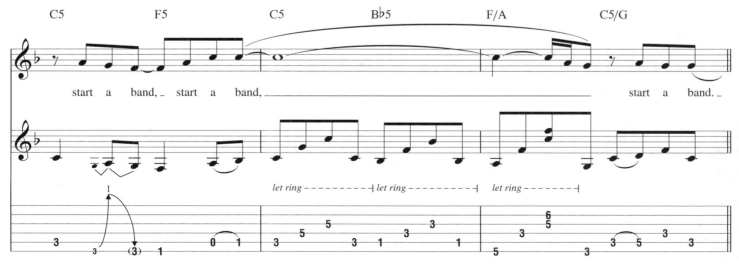

start a band, start a band, start a band.

Interlude

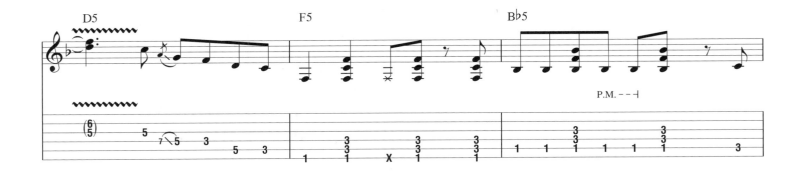

2. Now all those girls ___

Verse

_____ that were too cool to talk ___ to, they'll be wait - ing in a line out back. ___

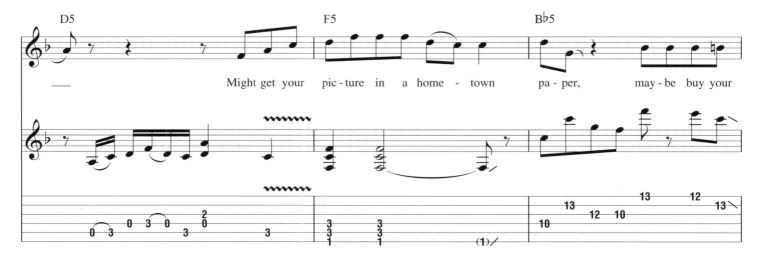

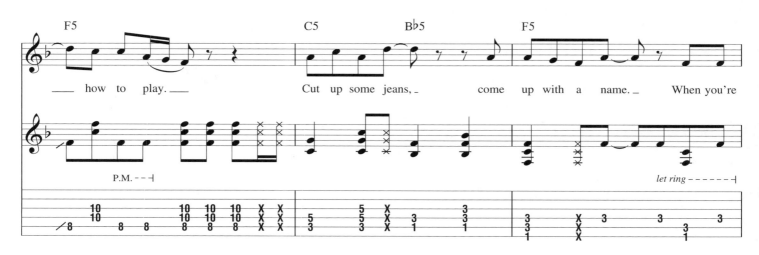

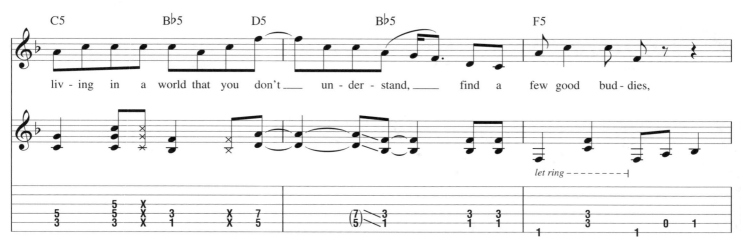

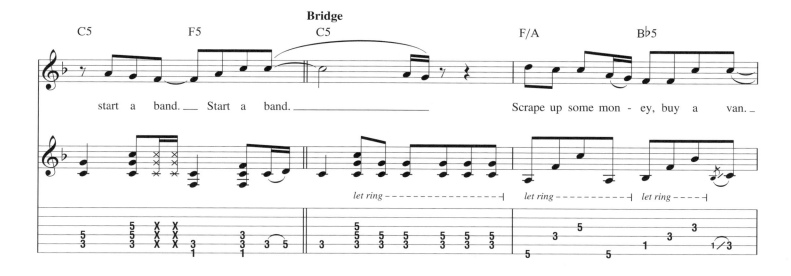

Bridge

start a band.___ Start a band._____ Scrape up some mon - ey, buy a van._

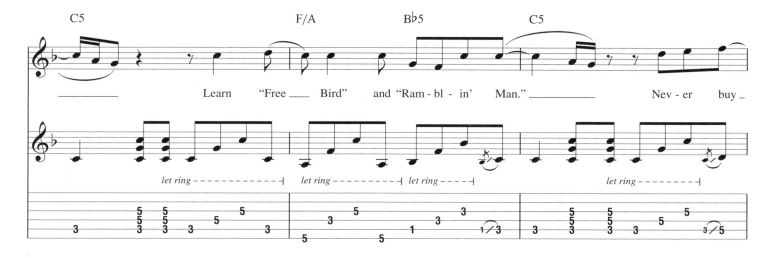

_____ Learn "Free ___ Bird" and "Ram - bl - in' Man."_____ Nev - er buy _

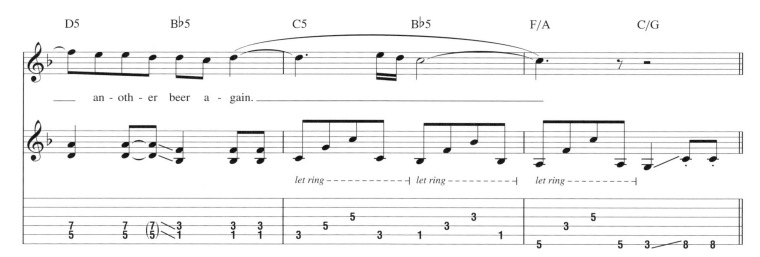

___ an - oth - er beer a - gain._____

Guitar Solo

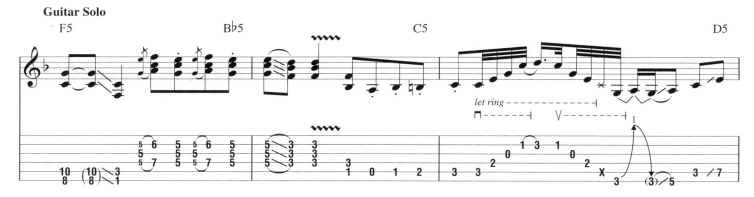

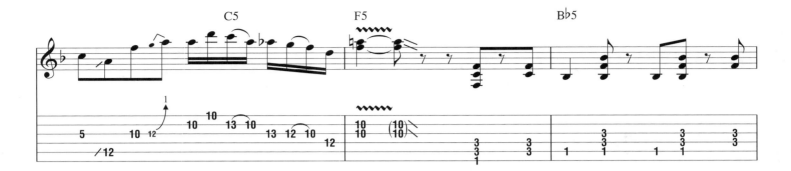

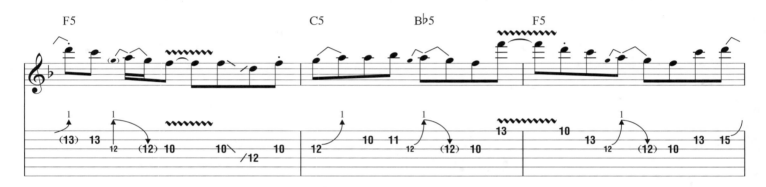

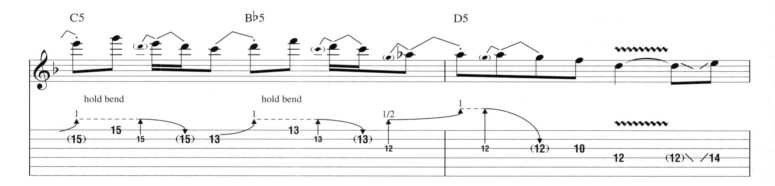

Chorus

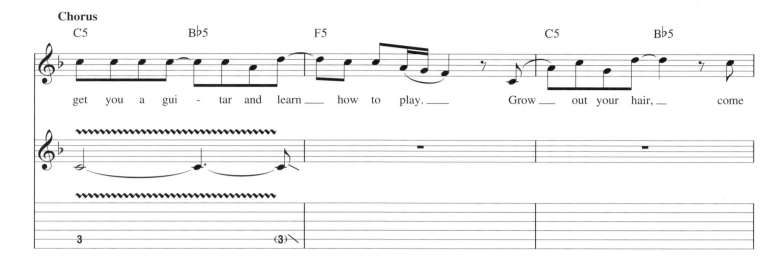

get you a gui - tar and learn___ how to play.___ Grow___ out your hair,___ come

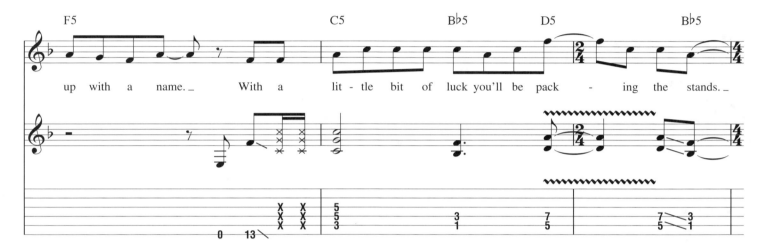

up with a name.___ With a   lit - tle bit of luck you'll be pack___ - ing the stands.___

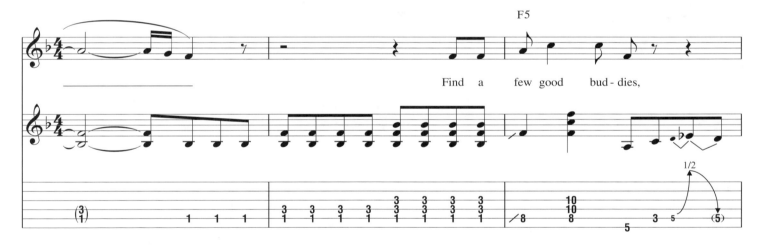

Find a   few good   bud - dies,

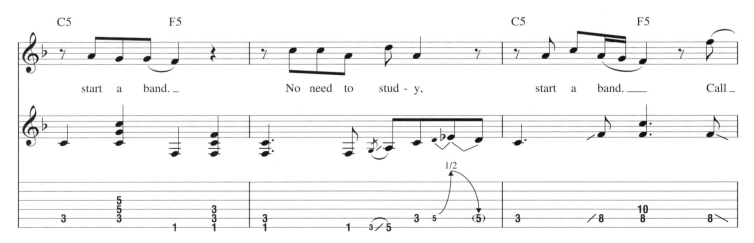

start a band.___   No need to   stud - y,   start a band.___   Call___

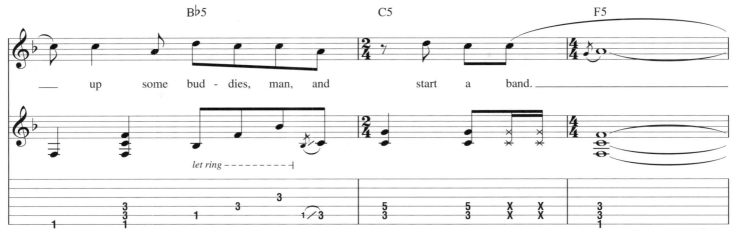

up some bud - dies, man, and start a band.

Guitar Solo

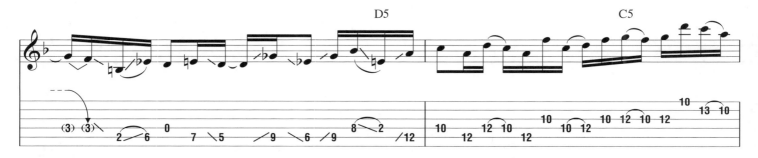

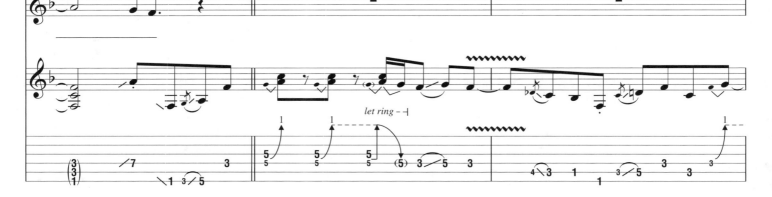

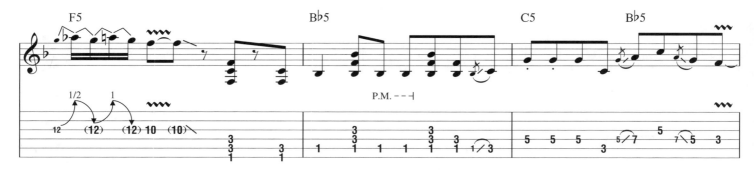

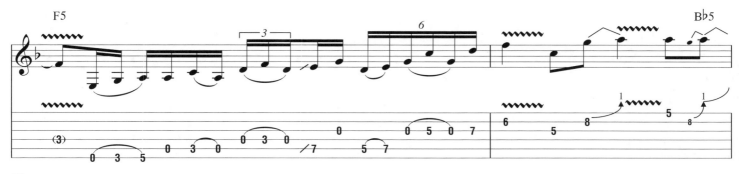

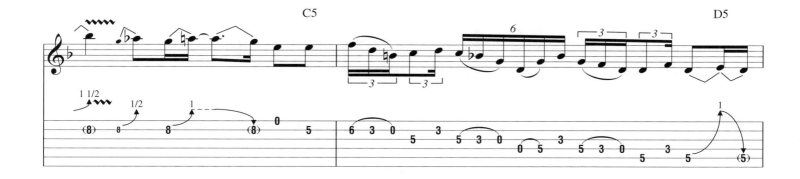

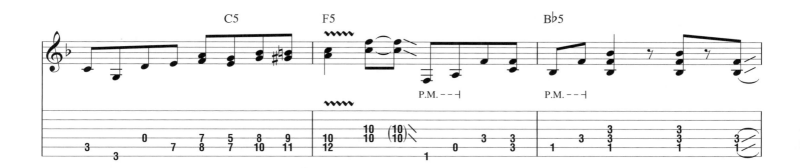

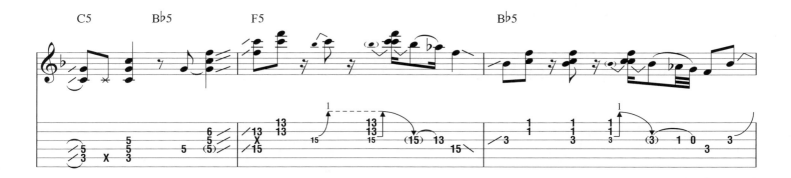

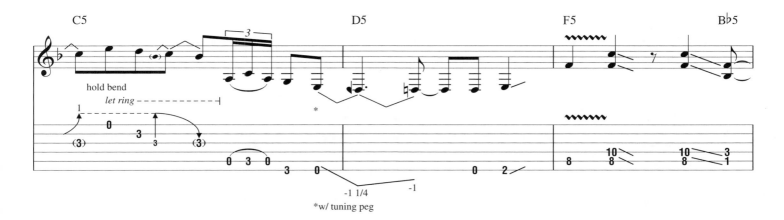

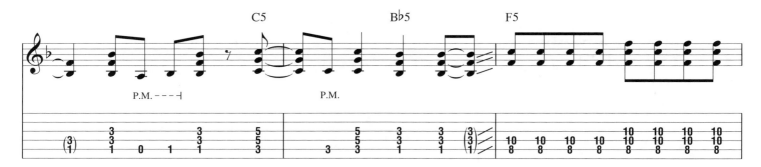

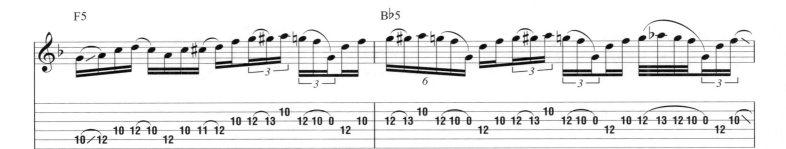

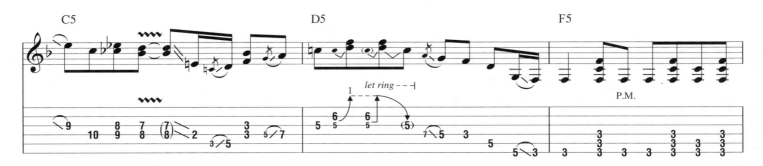

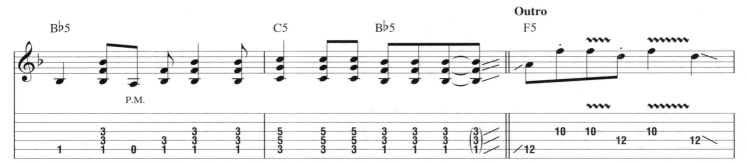

Outro

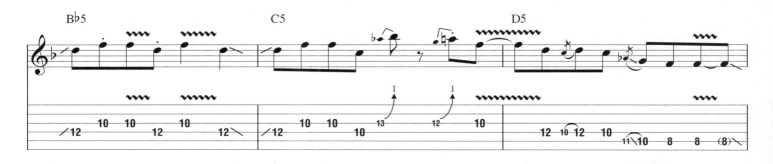

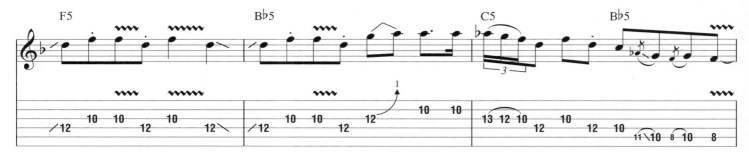

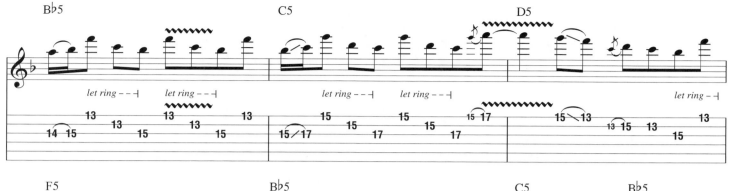

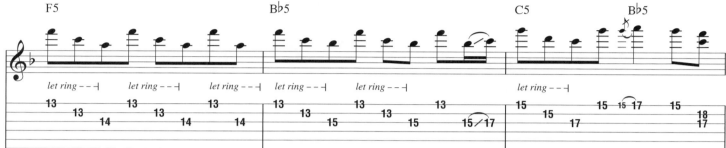

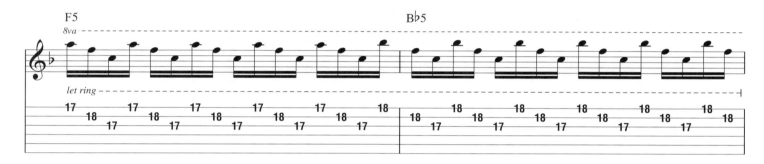

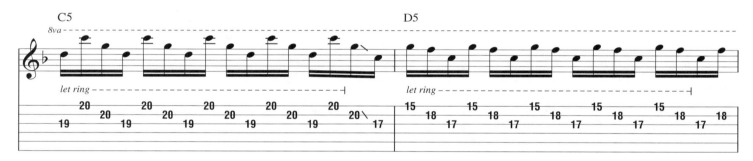

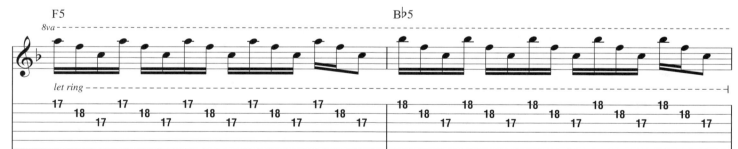

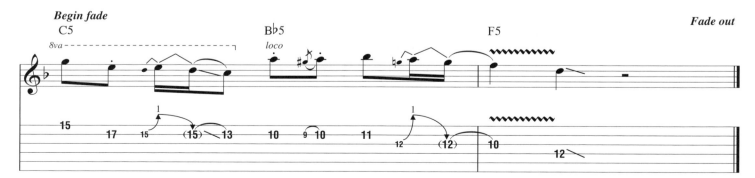

Ticks

Words and Music by Brad Paisley, Kelley Lovelace and Tim Owens

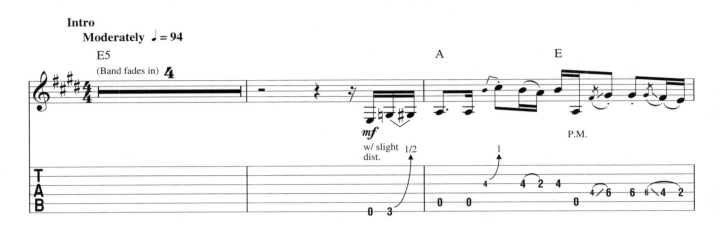

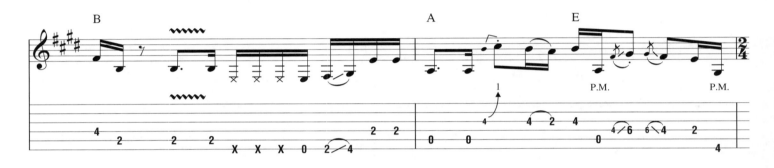

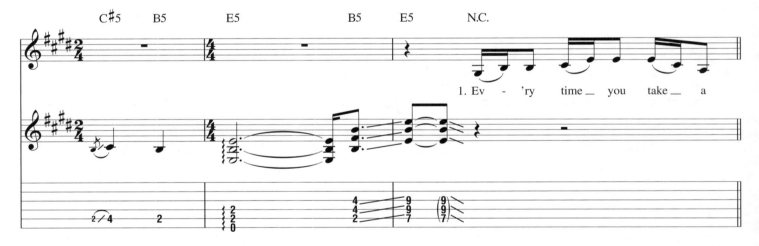

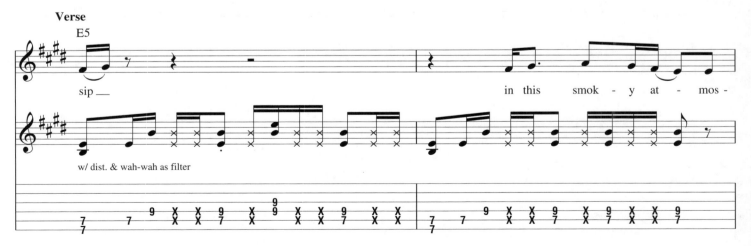

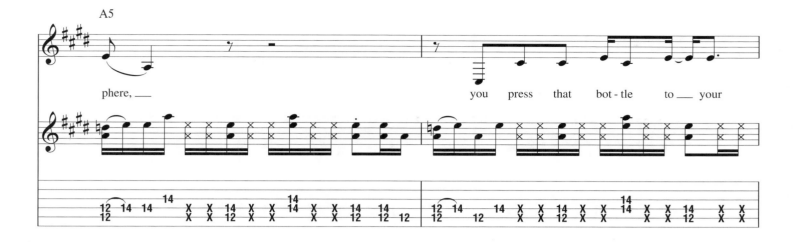

A5

phere, ___ you press that bot-tle to ___ your

E5

lips _____ and I wish I was ___ your

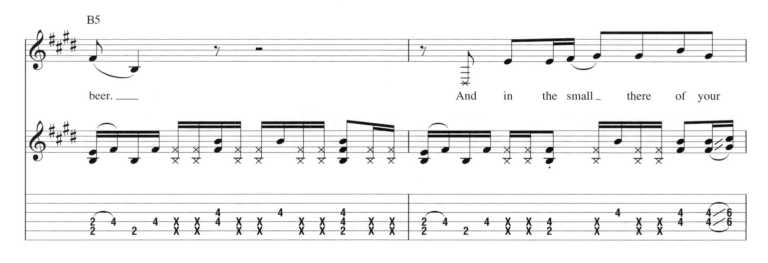

B5

beer. ___ And in the small ___ there of your

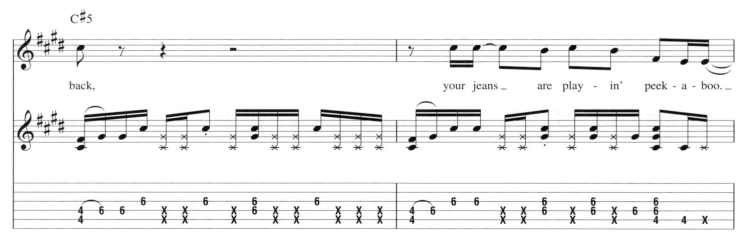

C#5

back, your jeans ___ are play-in' peek-a-boo. __

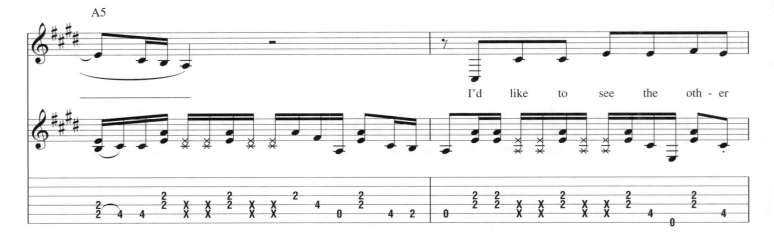

I'd like to see the oth- er

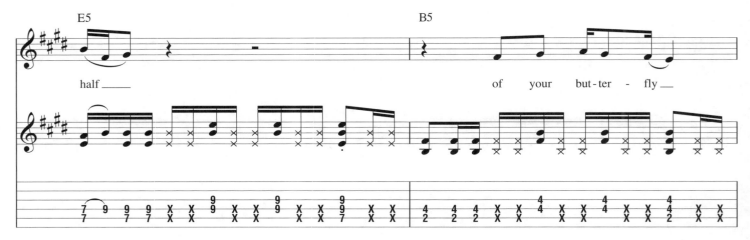

half _____ of your but- ter - fly _____

Pre-Chorus

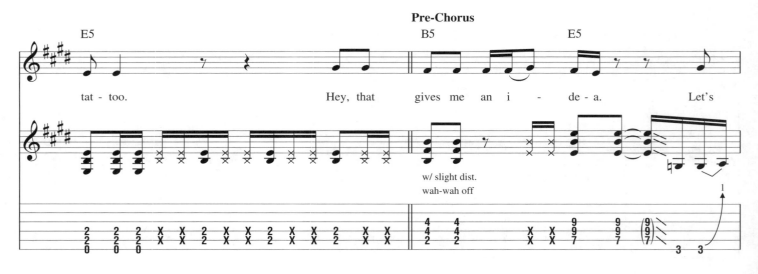

tat - too. Hey, that gives me an i - de - a. Let's

w/ slight dist.
wah-wah off

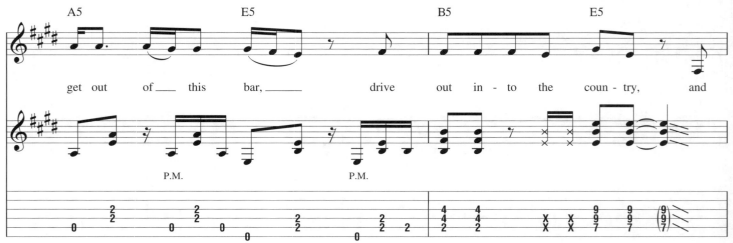

get out of ___ this bar, _____ drive out in - to the coun - try, and

P.M.   P.M.

𝄋 Chorus

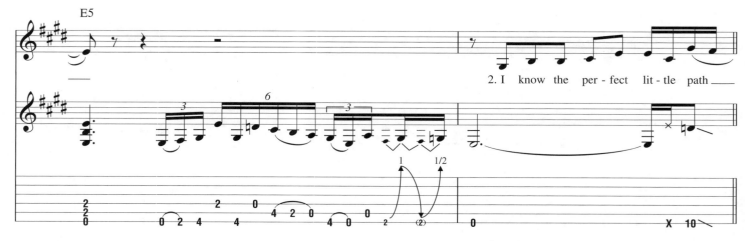

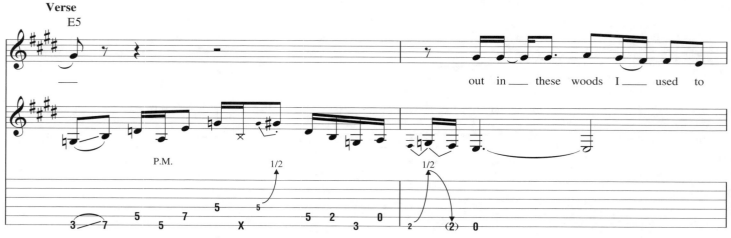

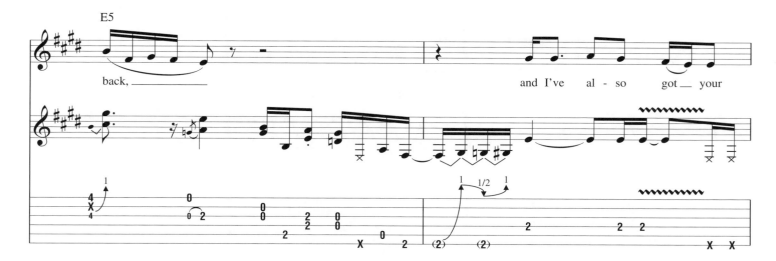

back, _____ and I've al - so got _ your

front. _____ I'd hate to waste a night _ like

this. _____ I'll keep you safe, you wait _ and see. _

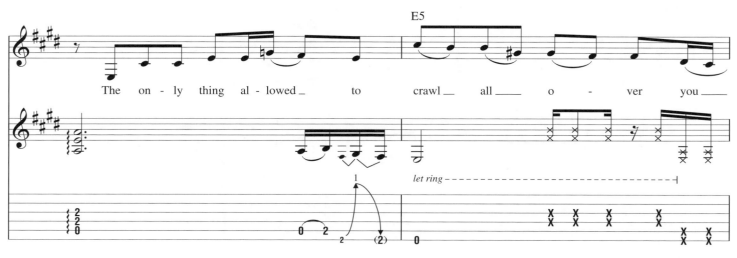

The on - ly thing al - lowed _ to crawl _ all _ o - ver you _

when we get ___ there ___ is ___ me. _____ You know, ___

Pre-Chorus

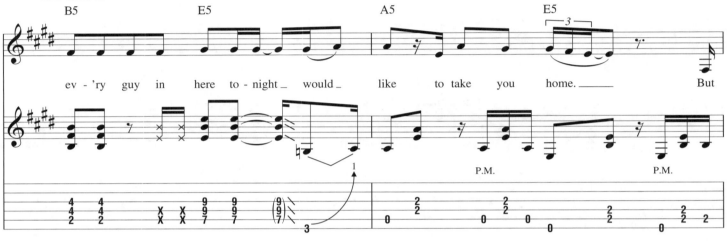

ev - 'ry guy in here to - night ___ would ___ like to take you home. ___ But

D.S. al Coda 1

I've got way more class than them. Babe, that ain't what I want. ___

Coda 1

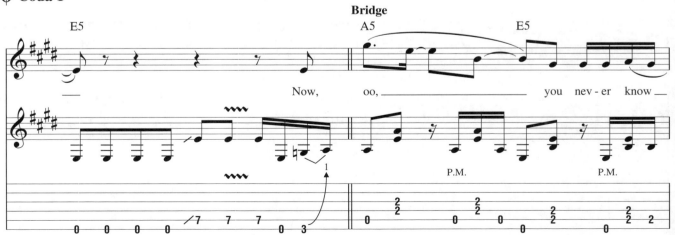

Bridge

Now, oo, _____ you nev - er know ___

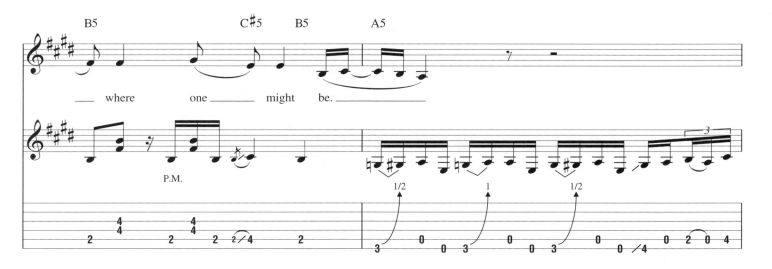

where one _____ might be. _____

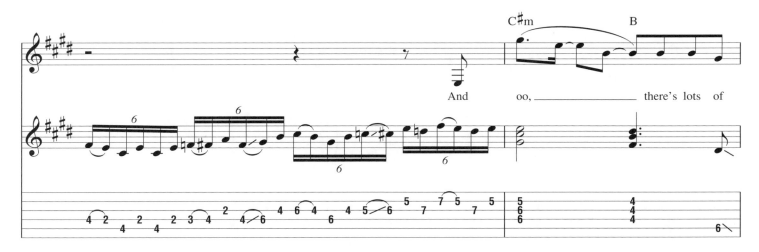

And oo, _____ there's lots of

plac - es that are hard _____ to reach. _____ I got - cha.

Guitar Solo

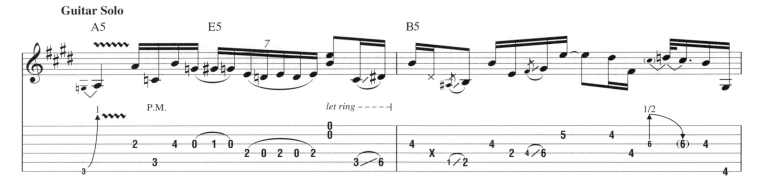

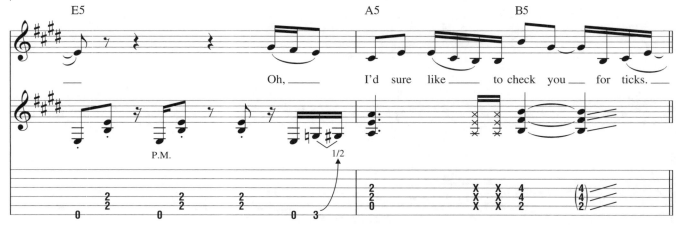

Coda 2

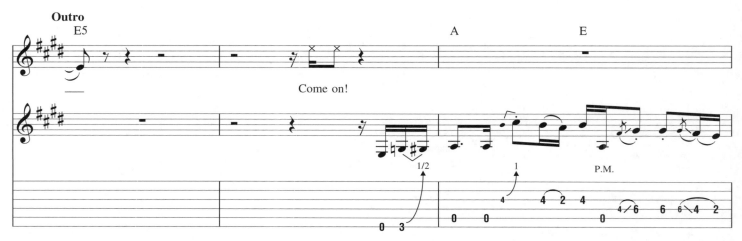

Oh, ____ I'd sure like ____ to check you ____ for ticks.

Outro

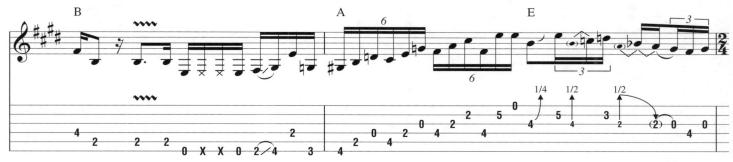

Come on!

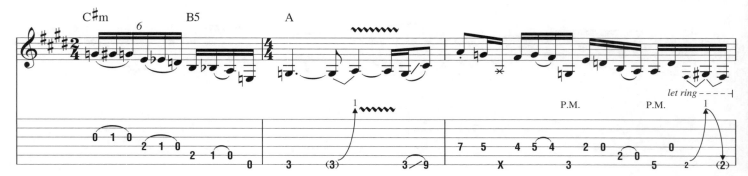

E5

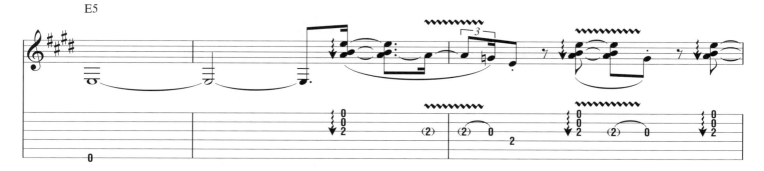

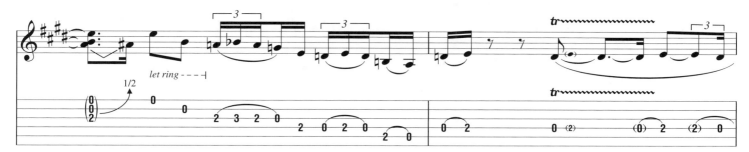

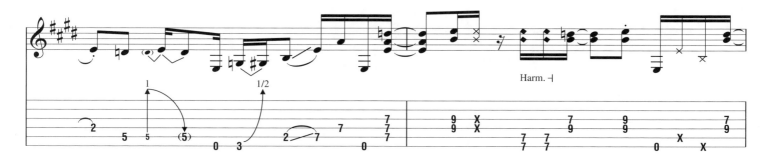

Begin fade

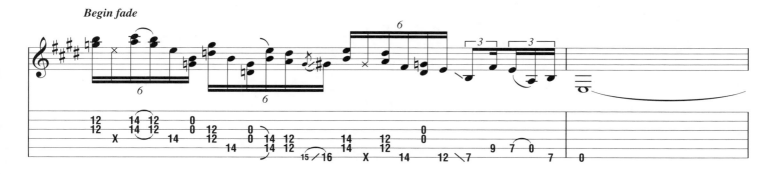

Fade out

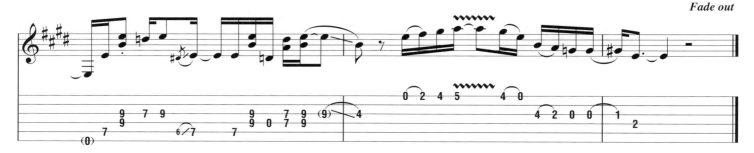

Time Warp

Words and Music by Brad Paisley and Frank Rogers

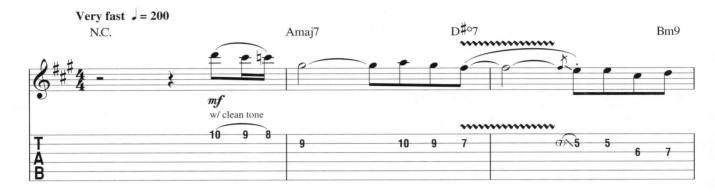

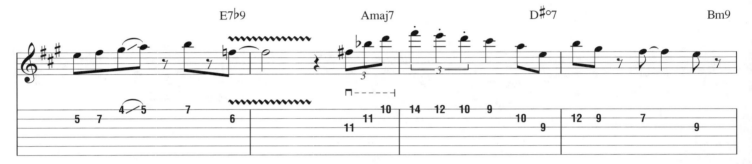

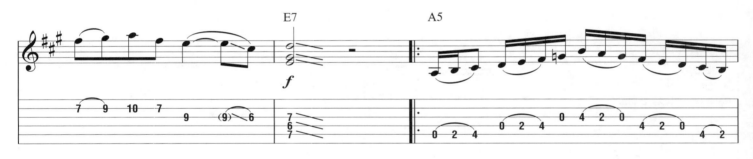

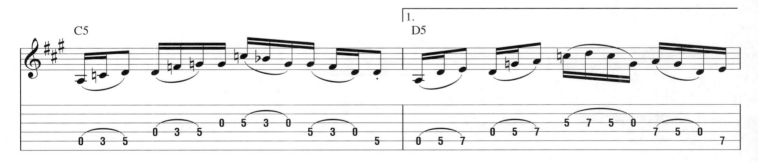

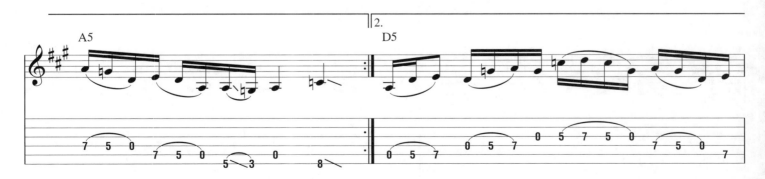

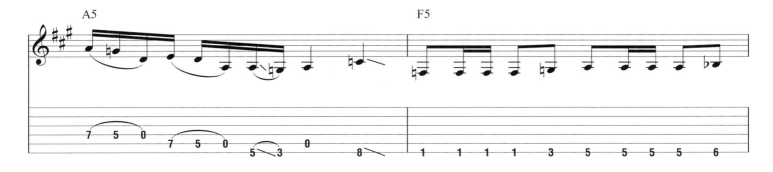

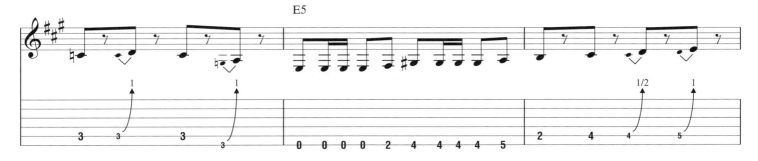

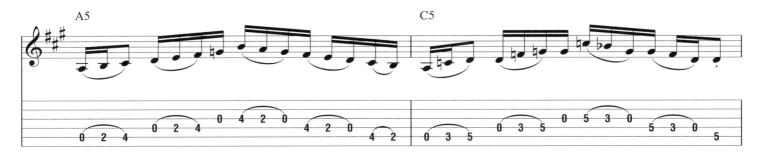

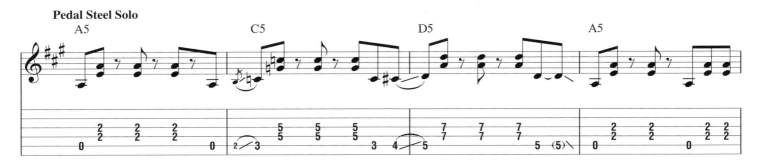

Pedal Steel Solo

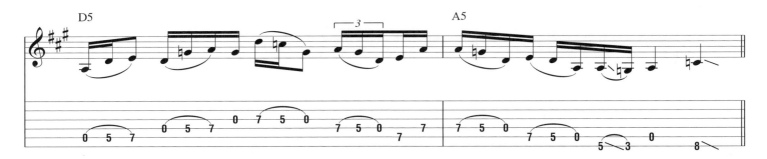

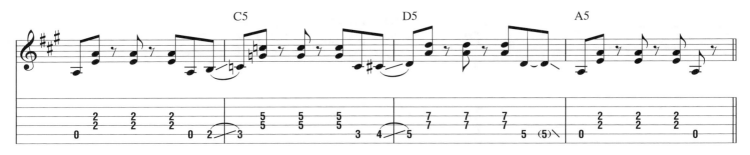

Fiddle Solo

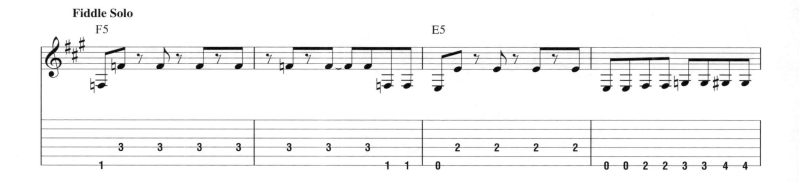

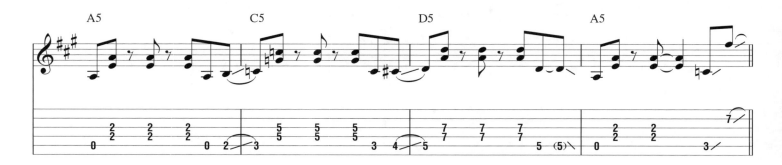

Guitar Solo

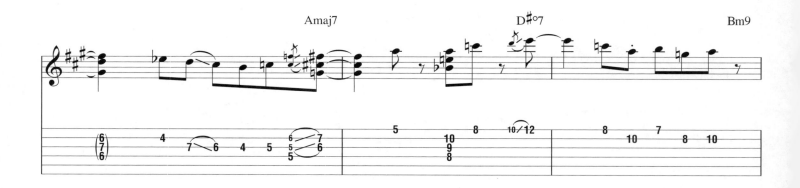

68

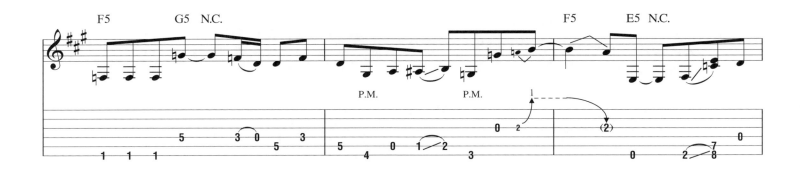

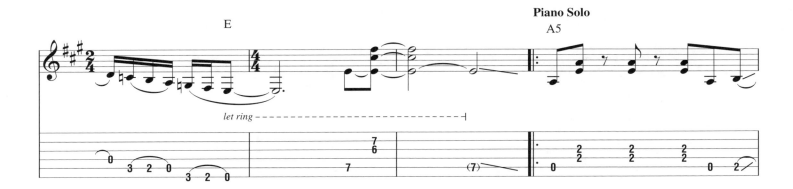

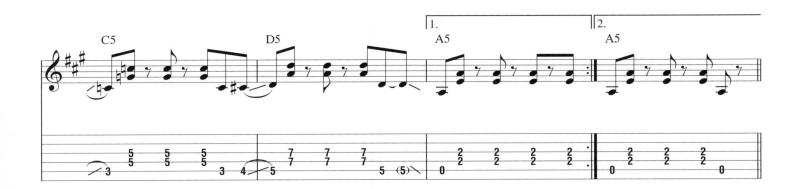

Guitar Solo

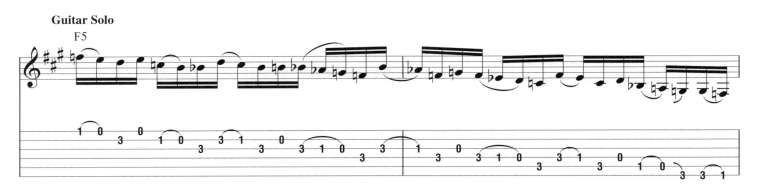

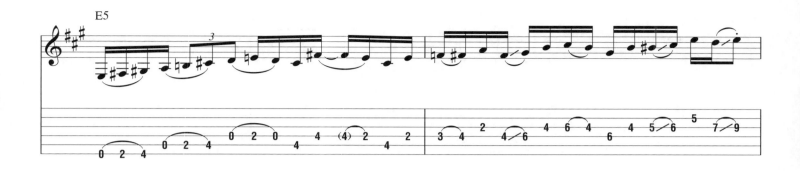

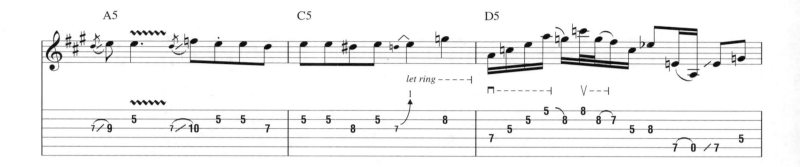

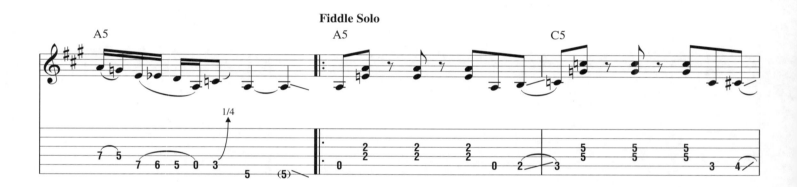

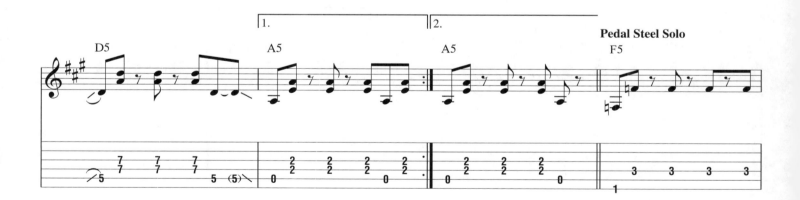

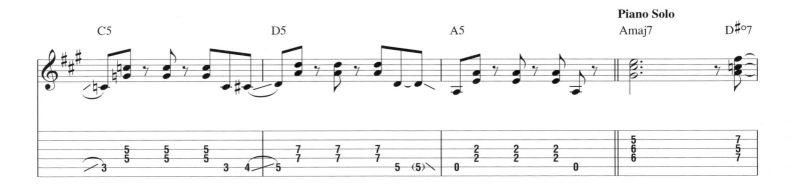

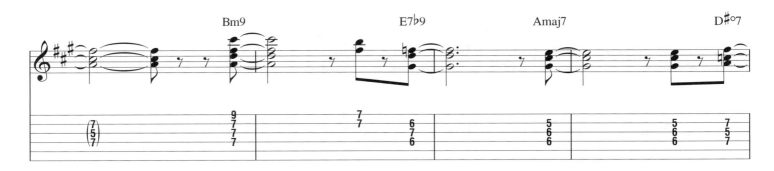

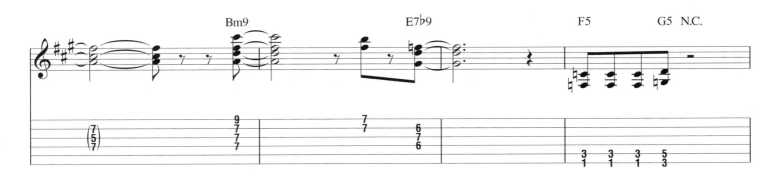

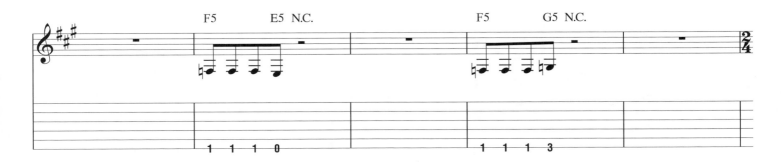

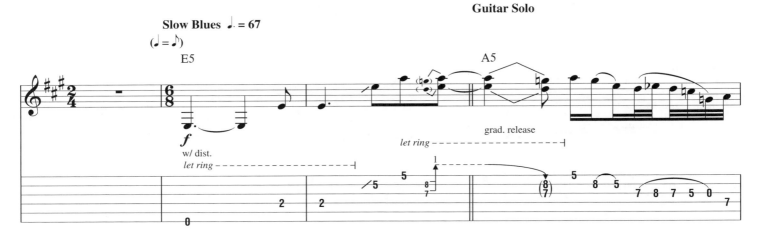

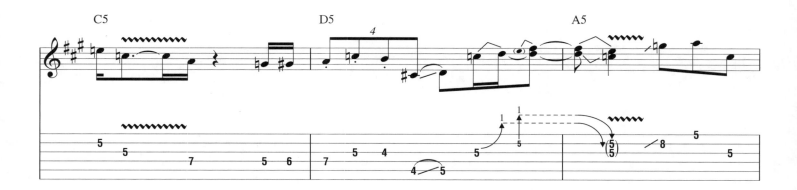

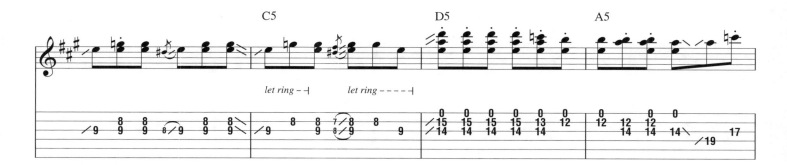

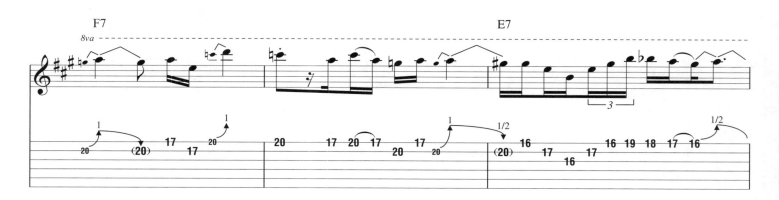

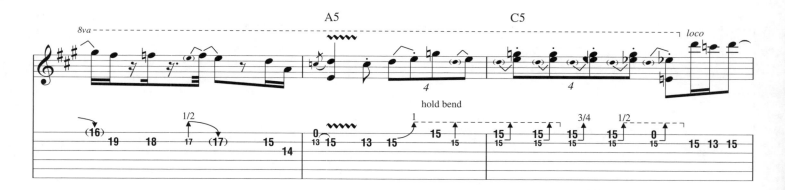

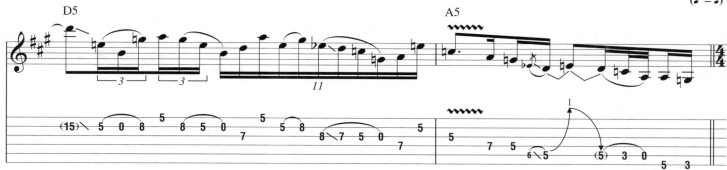

Fast ♩ = 200

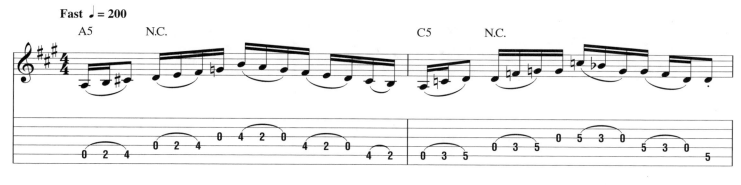

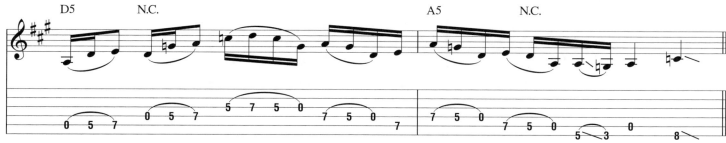

Guitar Solo

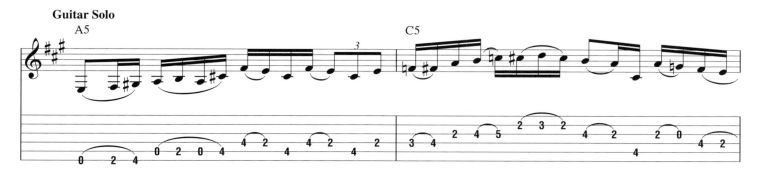

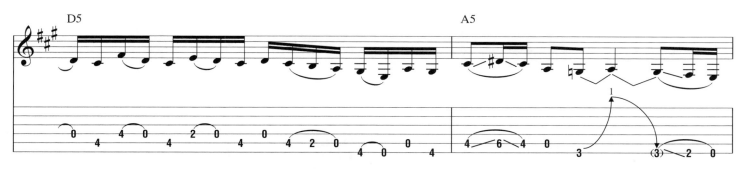

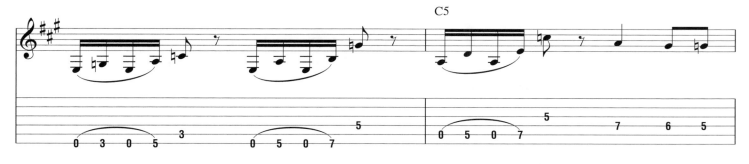

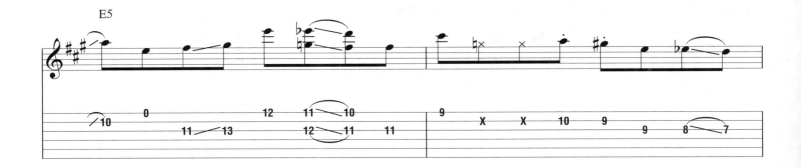

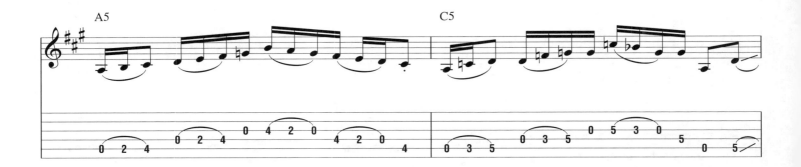

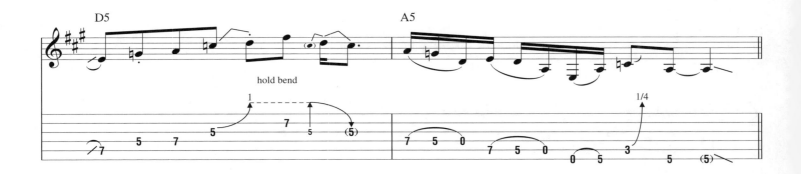

Bass Solo

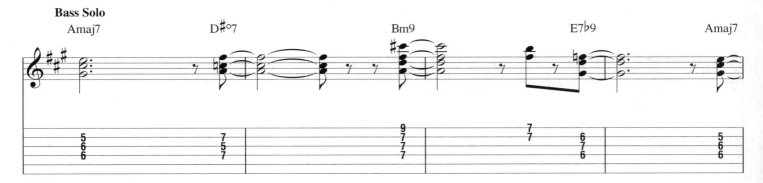

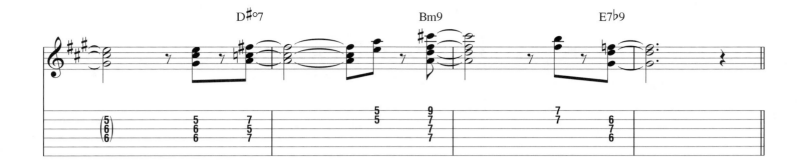

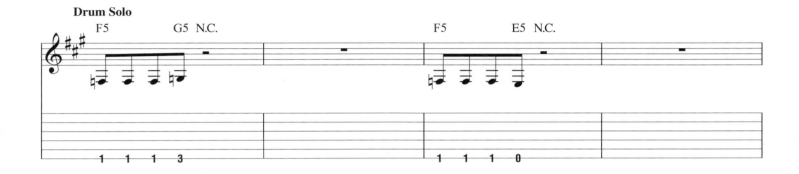

Drum Solo

Pedal Steel/Fiddle Solo

Piano Solo

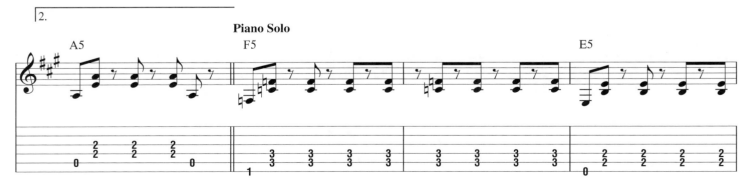

Guitar Solo

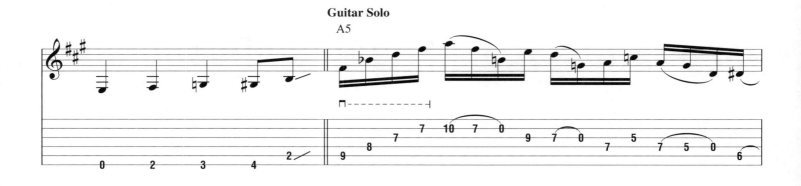

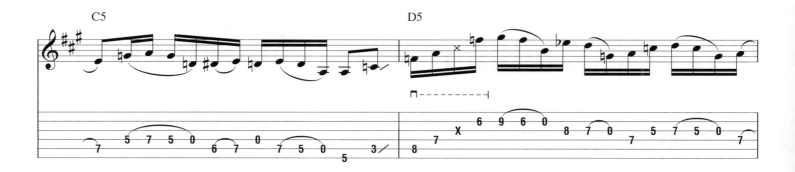

Outro

Free time

Shouted: Whoa!

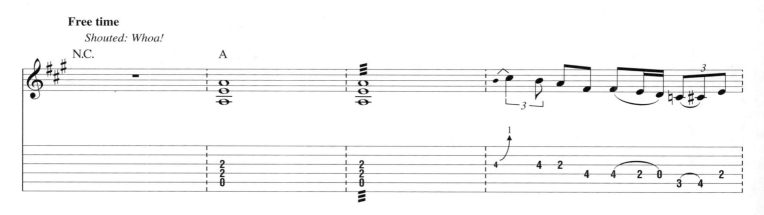

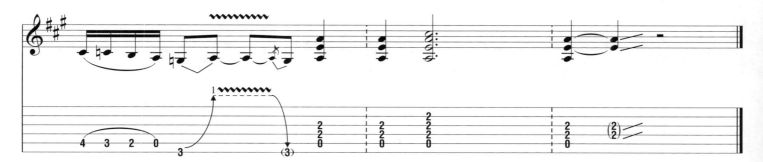

The World

Words and Music by Brad Paisley, Kelley Lovelace and Lee Thomas Miller

oth - er   check - in' ac - count.____   To the plumb - er that came ____ to - day _

2nd time, substitute Fill 1

____   you're just an - oth - er   house. _____   At the

Fill 1

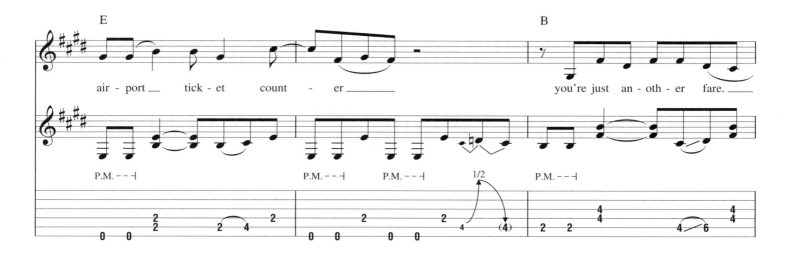

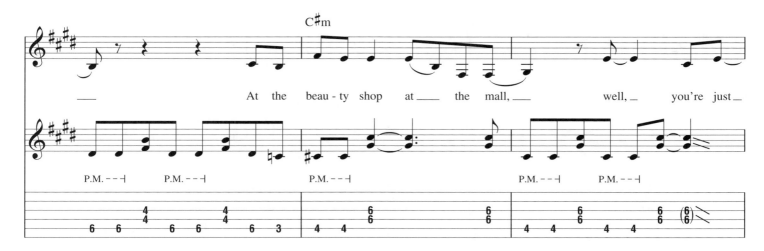

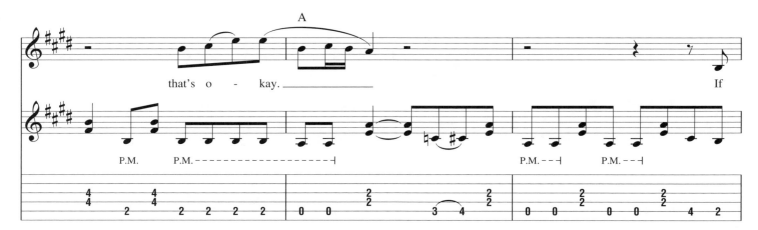

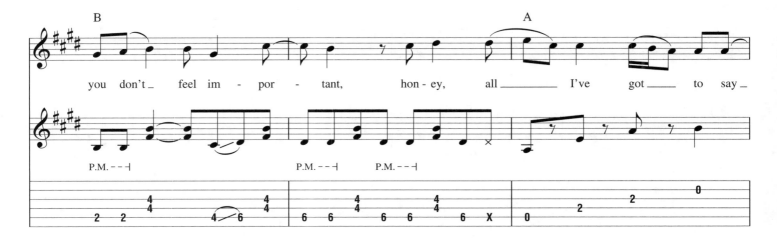

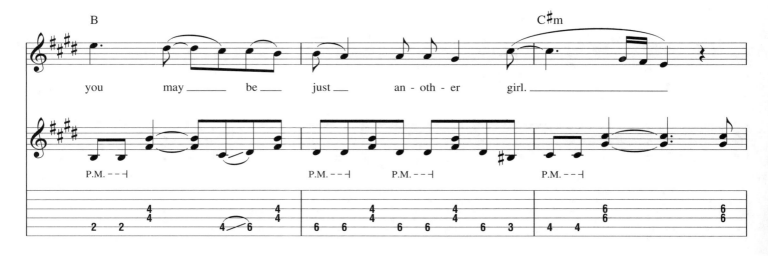

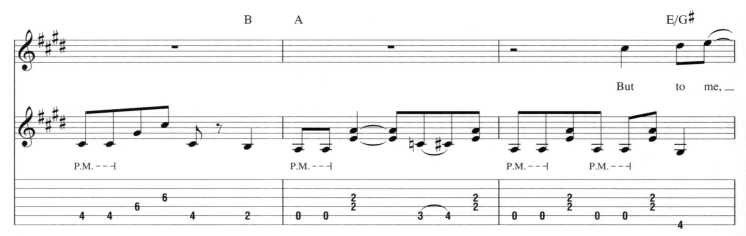

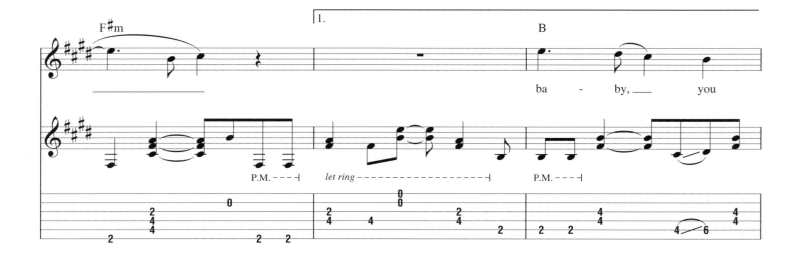

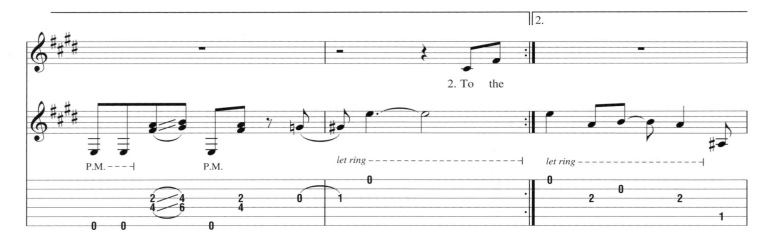

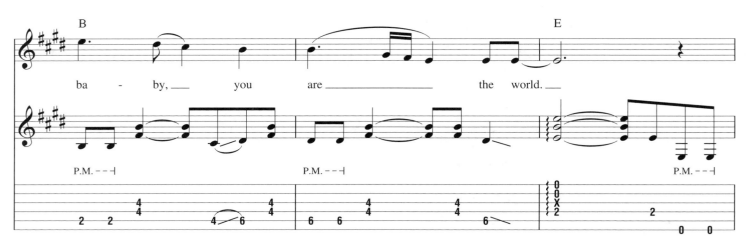

Bridge

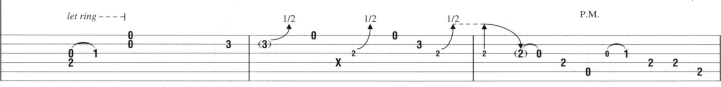

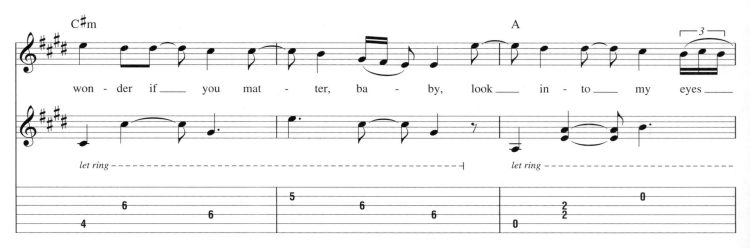

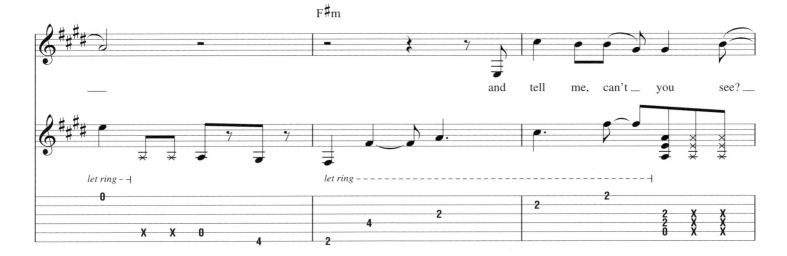

F#m

and tell me, can't _ you see? _

let ring

let ring

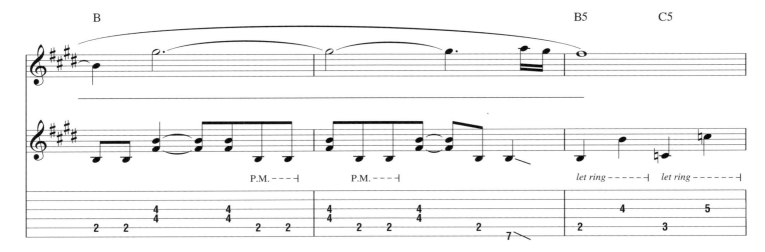

B

B5   C5

P.M.

P.M.

let ring   let ring

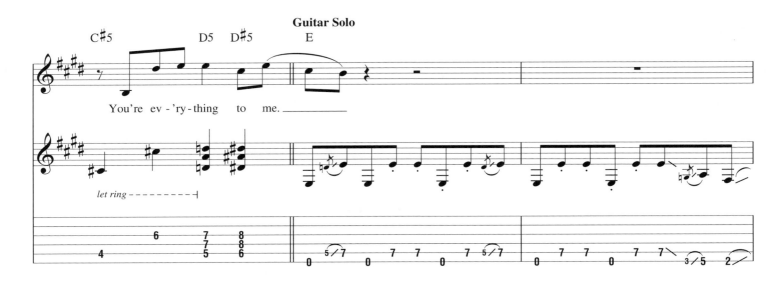

C#5   D5 D#5   E

Guitar Solo

You're ev-'ry-thing   to   me.

let ring

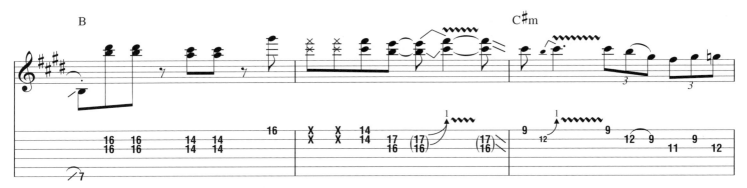

B

C#m

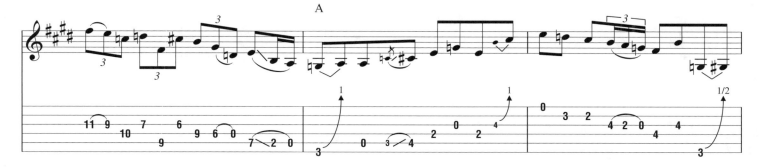

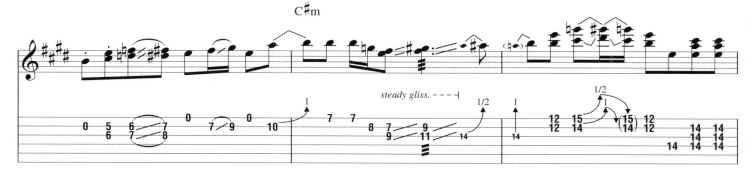

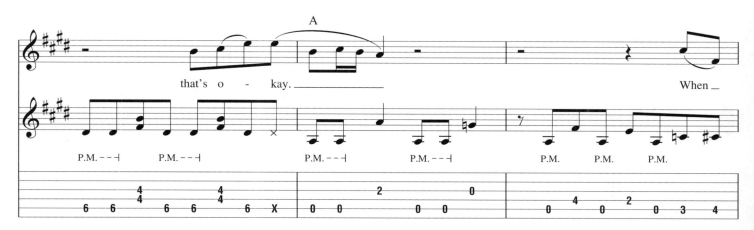

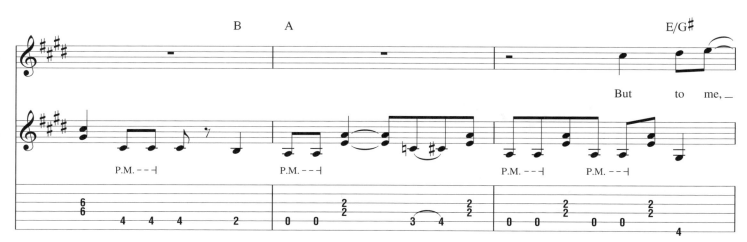

F#m

B

ba - by, ___ you

P.M. ---| let ring -----------| P.M. -----------|

Outro-Guitar Solo

E

1., 2., 3.

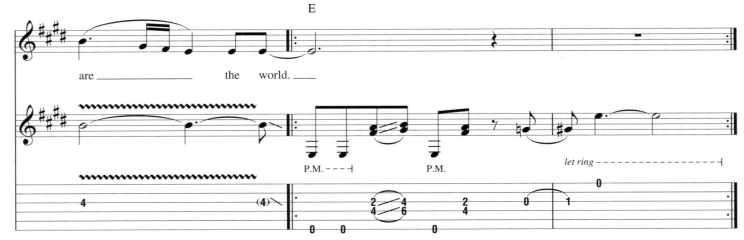

are _____ the world. ___

P.M. ---| P.M. let ring -----------|

4.

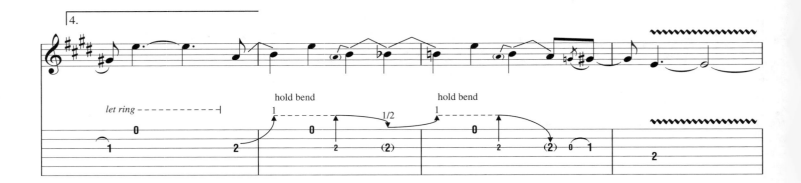

let ring --------| hold bend 1/2 hold bend

1/2

86

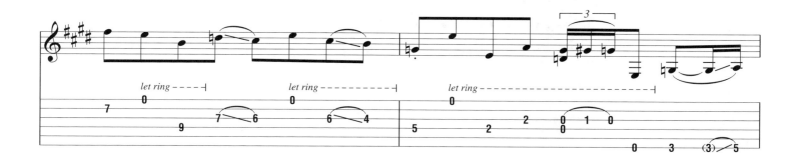

let ring - - - -
let ring - - - - - - - - - -
let ring -

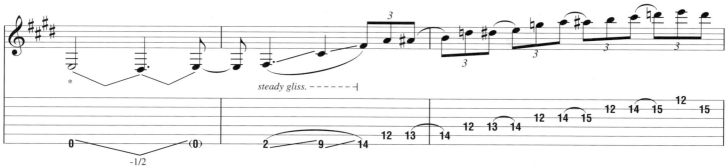

*
steady gliss. - - - - - - -

-1/2
*Push forward on neck.

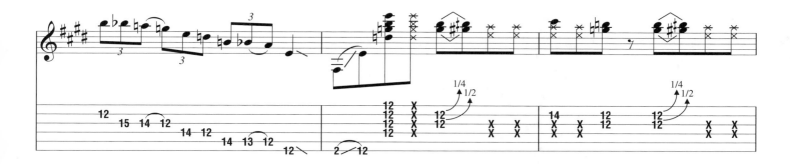

1/4
1/2

1/4
1/2

1/4
1/2

1/4
1/2

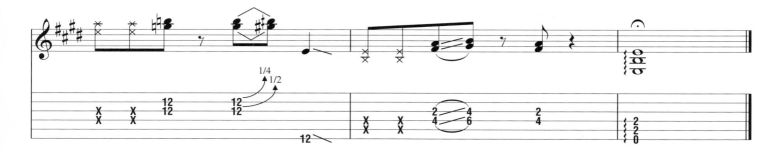

1/4
1/2

Additional Lyrics

2. To the waiter at the restaurant you're just another tip,
   To the guy at the ice cream shop you're just another dip.
   And you can't get reservations 'cause you don't have the clout,
   Or you didn't get an invitation 'cause somebody left you out.

GUITAR NOTATION LEGEND

THE MUSICAL STAFF shows pitches and rhythms and is divided by bar lines into measures. Pitches are named after the first seven letters of the alphabet.

TABLATURE graphically represents the guitar fingerboard. Each horizontal line represents a string, and each number represents a fret.

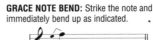

4th string, 2nd fret   1st & 2nd strings open, played together   open D chord

HALF-STEP BEND: Strike the note and bend up 1/2 step.

WHOLE-STEP BEND: Strike the note and bend up one step.

GRACE NOTE BEND: Strike the note and immediately bend up as indicated.

SLIGHT (MICROTONE) BEND: Strike the note and bend up 1/4 step.

BEND AND RELEASE: Strike the note and bend up as indicated, then release back to the original note. Only the first note is struck.

PRE-BEND: Bend the note as indicated, then strike it.

VIBRATO: The string is vibrated by rapidly bending and releasing the note with the fretting hand.

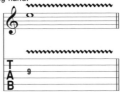

PALM MUTING: The note is partially muted by the pick hand lightly touching the string(s) just before the bridge.

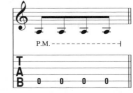

HAMMER-ON: Strike the first (lower) note with one finger, then sound the higher note (on the same string) with another finger by fretting it without picking.

PULL-OFF: Place both fingers on the notes to be sounded. Strike the first note and without picking, pull the finger off to sound the second (lower) note.

LEGATO SLIDE: Strike the first note and then slide the same fret-hand finger up or down to the second note. The second note is not struck.

SHIFT SLIDE: Same as legato slide, except the second note is struck.

TRILL: Very rapidly alternate between the notes indicated by continuously hammering on and pulling off.

TAPPING: Hammer ("tap") the fret indicated with the pick-hand index or middle finger and pull off to the note fretted by the fret hand.

NATURAL HARMONIC: Strike the note while the fret-hand lightly touches the string directly over the fret indicated.

PINCH HARMONIC: The note is fretted normally and a harmonic is produced by adding the edge of the thumb or the tip of the index finger of the pick hand to the normal pick attack.

TREMOLO PICKING: The note is picked as rapidly and continuously as possible.

VIBRATO BAR DIVE AND RETURN: The pitch of the note or chord is dropped a specified number of steps (in rhythm), then returned to the original pitch.

VIBRATO BAR SCOOP: Depress the bar just before striking the note, then quickly release the bar.

VIBRATO BAR DIP: Strike the note and then immediately drop a specified number of steps, then release back to the original pitch.

Additional Musical Definitions

(accent)   • Accentuate note (play it louder).

(staccato)   • Play the note short.

D.S. al Coda   • Go back to the sign (%), then play until the measure marked "*To Coda*," then skip to the section labelled "**Coda**."

D.C. al Fine   • Go back to the beginning of the song and play until the measure marked "*Fine*" (end).

Fill   • Label used to identify a brief melodic figure which is to be inserted into the arrangement.

N.C.   • Harmony is implied.

• Repeat measures between signs.

• When a repeated section has different endings, play the first ending only the first time and the second ending only the second time.